Discover Thai Cooking
Times Editions
1 New Industrial Road, Singapore 1953

© Times Editions 1988
Reprinted 1989

Colour separation by Sixty-Six Litho, Singapore
Typesetting by Superskill, Singapore
Printing and binding by Tien Wah Press, Singapore

First published in Great Britian in 1988 by
Ward Lock Limited, 8 Clifford Street, London, W1X 1RB, an Egmont Company.

ISBN : 0 7063 6648 4

Printed in Singapore

DISCOVER
THAI

COOKING

DISCOVER
THAI
COOKING

Written by
PIERRE CHASLIN
PIYATEP CANUNGMAI

Photographed by
LUCA INVERNIZZI TETTONI

Edited by
JULIA ROLES

WARD LOCK LIMITED · LONDON

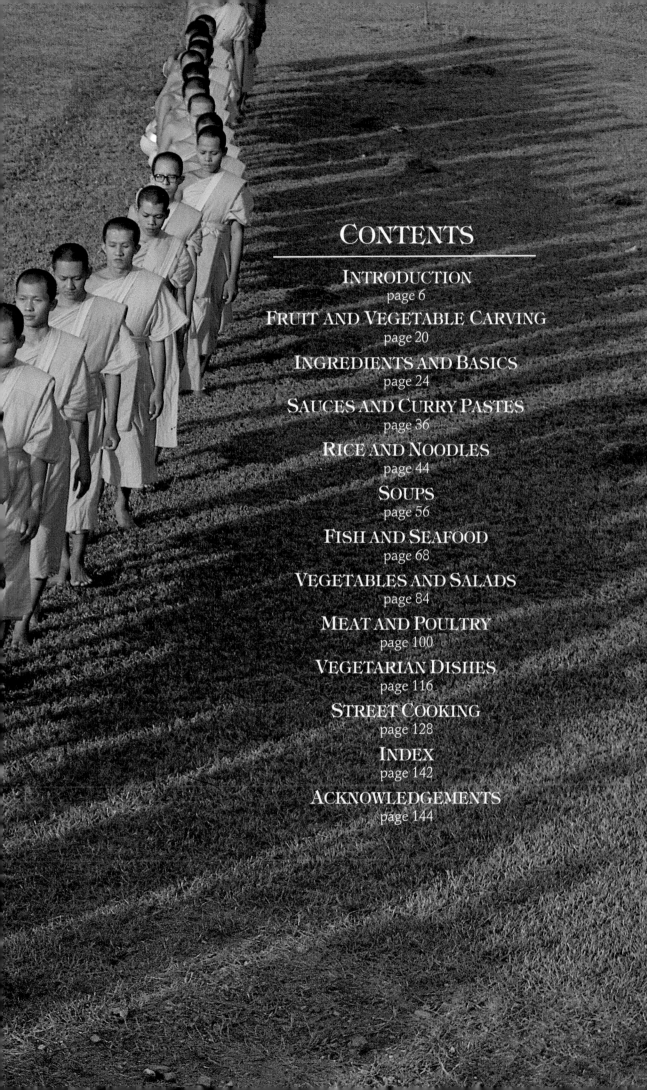

CONTENTS

INTRODUCTION

Southeast Asia was once known as "the golden cape" with Thailand being set like a powerful axe in the heart of this turbulent area. The history of Siam was built on rivalry and alternating victories and defeats in its battles with the Khmer empire, the kingdom of Luang Prabang in present-day Laos, and Burma. Today, Thailand has to reckon with less immediate but equally formidable neighbours like Vietnam and China.

A tropical climate dominates the whole country, with the central plains, the hilly north and the flat northeast sharing the same major seasons, but there are considerable variations caused by the nature of the land and its effects on the annual rainfall. It rains less in the north, the humidity level is higher in the Menam (Chao Phya) basin, and Bangkok can claim one of the world's shortest winters. Temperatures can reach 40°C (104°F) in the northeast during the hot season from March to May. The southwest monsoon brings the rainy season in June when temperatures drop slightly but humidity increases. November is the start of the cold season, especially in the mountainous north.

The mountains in the north and northwest belong to the same range as the Himalayas and constitute the last of its undulations towards the south. Reaching altitudes of between 1000 and 2000 metres (3300 and 6600 feet), this is an area of vast natural hardwood forests. In the large valleys rice is grown, and other crops include tobacco, coffee and tea. However, these cultivated lands represent no more than 6 per cent of the region. The rivers flowing

down from these northern valleys water the rich central plains, join briefly, then divide into two main arms. The larger branch goes through Bangkok and spreads itself towards the big deep port of Klong Toey, before finally reaching the Gulf of Thailand.

The admirably irrigated central plains which lend themselves naturally to the cultivation of rice, were chosen as the location for the establishment of the last three capitals of Siam. Ayuthaya, founded in the 14th century, remained the political centre of the country for four centuries until it was totally destroyed by the Burmese armies in 1767. Out of the disaster rose a young general called Phya Tak Sin, or Taksin as he was popularly known, who assembled an army and navy and expelled the Burmese from Ayuthaya. He immediately moved the capital downstream to a place called Thonburi on the west bank, where he was proclaimed king. He ruled until 1782, sadly degenerating from a strong and wise leader to a cruel and unjust tyrant. He was forced to abdicate and was executed. His place on the throne was taken by one of his brilliant and trusted generals, Chao Phya Chakri, establishing the Chakri dynasty which continues until today. The capital was then transferred across the river from Thonburi to Bangkok.

The northeast is the poorest part of Thailand, and the

Above: Ruins at Ayuthaya.

Right: Tending the rice at Nakhon Phanom in the poor northeast.

Left: Home for a wealthy Bangkok family.

Below: One of the many fine white beaches on the island of Phuket.

source of its biggest economic and social problems. The soil is thin and there is either not enough rain or too much. The Mekong can cause havoc when it floods but usually the rainy season is too short and the few rivers become narrow trickles of water during the dry season. The sandstone substratum retains very little water and this evaporates during the hot season so the rice yield depends totally on how much rain falls during the monsoon season. Moreover, the rice normally cultivated is a sticky rice unpopular for export. The population exists on an inadequate diet and in very poor conditions. The people thus become easy prey to false dreams about the big city and to the pressure of unscrupulous agents scouring the countryside for a naive and cheap work force. These northeasterners end up in the open-air bars of Pattaya, some "hot streets" of Bangkok, and menial factory jobs. Thousands of hands, worn out by the land, wash the laundry, cook the food and do the housework for the well-off Bangkokians.

The picture is rosier in the south of Thailand, the handle of the axe which is blessed with plentiful rainfall and lush tropical vegetation. The cultivation of rubber, introduced when the century was young, has been extensively developed to supplement the basic wealth which stems from the mining of tin, refined at Phuket. This refinery is not much appreciated by the tourists who come to the island to enjoy the natural beauty of its white beaches, and who are making an increasingly important contribution to the economy of the area.

The Thais, Who Are They?

But the Thais, who are they? For centuries known as Siamese, their name was changed in 1940 by the new democratic government in order to bring together all those of the same language group. But Thai or Siamese, who are these Orientals who have managed to avoid European colonization in the 19th century and communist conquerors in the 20th?

A visitor, freshly arrived, might consider that Thailand is populated by a single race where one can only distinguish the very rich from the very poor. But, after some time, on closer acquaintance, the features that separate the ethnic groups from each other become more obvious.

What is surprising, at first, is the importance of the Chinese community. The Chinese, with their fairer skin, rounder faces and less athletic bodies, make up a large proportion of the Bangkok population. Industrious, dynamic, prosperous and noisy, Chinatown is their village, the whole city is their empire. Everywhere we see the development of condominiums, commercial centres and first-class hotels born from their passion for work and their commercial acumen.

This population did not come recently. The Theravada Buddhism practised in Thailand encourages believers to turn away from materialism in order to achieve salvation and real happiness. As a result, peasants are content to live at subsistence level, while educated Thais aim at being civil

Above: Buddhist monks sharing a simple meal.

Right: A street in Bangkok's Chinatown.

servants and teachers, the only way for them to achieve power with honour. The Chinese have long filled the gaps left in trade and industry. As far back as the 13th century, Chinese potters were encouraged to work in the capital, then Sukhothai. Later, the Chinese were allowed to mine for tin in the south of the country. In the next capital, Ayuthaya, Chinese merchants built residences more beautiful than those of their Indian and Arab colleagues. When the capital was established at Bangkok, the site the king wanted for his Grand Palace was already occupied by Chinese shops. He moved them a few kilometres down the riverbank to form what has now become Yaowaraj, the Chinatown of Bangkok. The first kings of the Chakri dynasty encouraged the Chinese immigration. They saw it as a source of income by taxation, thereby enriching the royal treasury and the war chest, while at the same time, giving a boost to commerce and export. Tempted by the prospect of huge profits, the Chinese began to pour into the country. These newcomers engaged promptly in the trade of pepper, sugar cane, cotton and other raw materials in high demand for export. Above all, they practically monopolized the rice trade and they were never to give up this position of commercial leadership. They have also made important contributions to Thai cuisine. Noodle and poultry dishes, and the use of soya sauce, are a few of the better-known elements of this legacy.

The Indians form a small minority group but the cultural influences from India have been considerable. They gave Theravada Buddhism to the Thais and they also gave

them the Hindu epic, the *Ramayana*, which the Thais renamed the *Ramakien*. The *Ramayana* tells of Rama who was one of the incarnations of the Hindu god, Vishnu, and who symbolizes virtue, and the victory of good over evil. The *Ramayana* forms the basis for the moral code in much of Asia, even to an extent in Buddhist Thailand where the kings of the Chakri dynasty have adopted the name Rama, the present sovereign being Rama IX. An Indian language, Pali, is used for Buddhist texts and prayers, the Thai vocabulary has been enriched by Sanskrit, and Thai cuisine by the Indian love of spices and curries.

The southern people are of Malay origin and have darker skin, frizzier hair and rounder eyes than the Thais. Living mainly in the four most southerly provinces near the border with Malaysia, they are linked to their Malaysian neighbours by a common Islamic faith. This has led to a radical Muslim separatist movement which would like to see these provinces attached to Malaysia and which causes occasional problems for the Thai government. In this part of the country the Buddhist temples are replaced by mosques,

and rice paddies give way to coconut, rubber and pineapple plantations. "Satay" — skewers of meat, poultry or fish cooked over charcoal and served with a peanut sauce — comes from this area, as well as a taste for spicy food using generous amounts of curcuma or turmeric.

And the Thais themselves in this melting pot? They make up 90 per cent of the population, but where did they come from? How did they manage to establish the kingdom that we know today? A Thai ethnic group appears in Chinese chronicles as early

Lisu women and men in their traditional costumes.

as the 6th century. They are found in the area southeast of the Yangtze, and then again, two centuries later, in the high valleys of Yunnan, China's most southern province. Did the Thais move in large numbers to Southeast Asia under pressure from the Mongols who were annexing the Yunnan territory? Or did they move naturally with the flow of water, going further south in a migratory movement which seems typical of the area? The question marks cannot be totally eliminated and the excavations at Ban Chiang in northeast Thailand have revealed the existence here of a culture thousands of years earlier than this. Indian influence is thought to have started as early as the 3rd century BC and the Mons and Khmers were the first Indianized peoples to settle in what is now Thailand. One thing is clear, however, and that is that the Thais went on carving their country at the expense of the Mons, the Burmans and the Khmers. They also integrated and combined with many heterogeneous elements including the Khmer communities in the northeast and the east, and the Mons along the Chao Phya river.

In the areas bordering Burma and Laos roam nomadic tribal groups — the Karen in the north and the west, and the Hmong, Yao, Akha, Lisu and Lahu in the north. Many of these hilltribes have come to Thailand from China relatively recently, and although they are being affected by increasing contact with the Thai culture, they retain their own traditions, religions and ways of life. Larp, dried meat, jasmine-flavoured rice and sticky rice are some of the culinary contributions of these different groups. But a more sinister product of the north comes from the poppy grown in the sadly famous golden triangle. This black area of economic activity is fought by the King and Queen themselves who take personal interest in developing alternative sources of income for the tribes.

Giant Buddhas, clouds of incense, graceful gestures.

Sanuk And Sabai

Religion and Royalty are the reasons for festival after festival, as well as for much of the beauty of Thailand with its unique heritage and culture – the golden palaces, temples and royal barges; the giant Buddhas dominating the faithful with their submissive sweetness; the clouds of incense drifting heavenwards from the worshippers; the richly adorned dancers; the graceful gestures; the serene faces. There is a temple in each neighbourhood and every village. Often the village is built within the walls of the temple. In this way sacred and secular lives are deeply intertwined. Some ceremonies follow the lunar calendar while others commemorate episodes in the life of the Buddha.

During these festivals the Thais demonstrate their taste for simple pleasures enjoyed in a crowd. What they enjoy more than anything else is "sanuk", their word for "fun", although the translation does not convey anything like its full meaning or the importance it plays in Thai life. Their love of "sanuk", their "joie de vivre", affects every aspect of their daily existence and reveals not an inability to face up to unpleasant realities but rather a determination to get as much pleasure as possible out of everything. This joyful serenity is called "sabai". Life's experiences are divided into those that are "sanuk" and those which are not. Eating definitely comes into the "sanuk" category which is why food vendors' stalls are such hives of activity in the huge bazaars that overwhelm the temples at festival time.

A pastime much loved by the Thais is to go "pai thiaw" which again is difficult to translate but roughly means to go for a stroll, wandering from place to place to see what's going on. Unlike most Westerners, the average Thai does not feel that every activity must have a particular purpose and, except in a monastery, he cannot understand the desire for solitude. He is never happier than amid the noise of a large crowd where he gets a feeling of companionship and of belonging. While drifting around, he might sample some tasty sweetmeat and will probably take some home since Thais like nothing better than a spontaneous and casual meal.

Thai cuisine is essentially very simple and the main ingredients are rice, vegetables, fish and spices. There are not many dishes which are considered appropriate only at certain times of the day, and meals will generally consist of rice accompanied by one or two dishes. The unmistakably Thai flavour comes from the combination of chilies, garlic, onions and shallots, coconut cream, coriander, basil, shrimp paste (kapi) and soya sauce. Despite the historical influences from India and China, Thai cooking is unique in its particular blending of these flavours. It can also be commended as a "nouvelle cuisine" as there is very little fat, and meat does not feature strongly. The food is lightly cooked, remains crunchy with all the nutritional value and flavour intact, and is then served in carefully measured quantities.

For a quick meal rural Thais like lightly cooked or raw vegetables, served with "nam prik" — a chili sauce mixed with shrimp paste — and accompanied by grilled fish. These dishes are easy to prepare and the ingredients are easily available — vegetables grow in the garden and fish are plentiful in nearby rivers. In the cities, breakfast is often obtained from the soup or noodle vendor, and lunch of rice and curry is also eaten in

Above: Plentiful supplies of fish in a Thai market.

Left: A floating chili stall.

Monks receiving their day's food from devout almsgivers.

the street or a nearby coffee shop. The evening meal is eaten with the family, usually at home, but special evenings are spent in huge open restaurants full of noise and smells, the food accompanied by plenty of beer or Mekong, the local whisky. The day usually ends as it began, with a bowl of satisfying "khao tom" or rice soup.

Tomorrow the women must be up early to prepare food to fill the begging bowls of the monks who will come by, as always, in the first light of dawn. The donors, who wait outside their homes for the saffron-clad men to come quietly past, do not expect or receive thanks from the monks and, indeed, it is the donors who are grateful, for the monks have given them an opportunity to earn merit by doing good to those in the Buddha's service. Female alms-givers must take care not to touch any part of the monk or his garments as they place food in his "batr" or bowl. The monks eat only what they receive in alms from the faithful and they have just two meals a day – one early in the morning and one before noon.

Even in more complicated meals for special occasions, the actual cooking time for Thai dishes is rarely longer than ten minutes. In most cases the ingredients can be prepared in advance, leaving the cooking until just before the meal time. The skill lies in the preparation of the ingredients. Thai cooks are expert in the handling of cutting tools and are unbeatable in the art of slicing, cutting and carving vegetables and meat. An unwritten rule in Thai cooking requires that each morsel of meat or fish, when eaten with half a spoonful of rice, makes just one mouthful. If the mouthful includes meat and vegetables together, then the pieces must be cut even smaller. The origins of this rule lie in the absence of knives, a symbol of aggression, at meal times. Well-sharpened knives are obviously vital to the Thai cook, and of almost equal importance are the pestle and mortar, used for pounding and

Left: Thai cooking utensils.

Below: A spirit house decorated for a festive occasion.

crushing the spices and other condiments. The cooking is usually done in a wok – a deep cone-shaped pan placed over gas or coals.

Official invitations to a meal are rare in Thailand. Friends drop in, unannounced, for a chat, and if conversation runs into a meal time, they are automatically asked to join in. In the north and northeast a pitcher of water is always placed in front of the house for the benefit of a thirsty traveller. A little more rice than is required is usually cooked in case an unexpected guest arrives. There is rarely any formal protocol at table and eating is delightful for its simplicity. The sort of heavy etiquette-bound entertaining so frequent in the West is unknown amongst the Thais. Tables and chairs are often absent, and everyone gathers round a mat on the floor, the men sitting cross-legged, the women with their legs tucked behind them so that feet are always pointing away from the group. Everyone takes a shower before-hand, if possible – cleanliness is godliness in Thailand, especially at meal times – but clothes are casual, usually sarongs or house dresses. Plates, bowls, forks and spoons are placed at random on the mat. The dishes arrive in no particular order and often all at once; rice, fish, meat, vegetables and soup can all be eaten at any time throughout the meal. Serving spoons are rare and the diners dip into the dishes with their own spoons, just as each mouthful is dipped into communal sauce bowls. There is great joy in the sharing.

The Thais are naturally graceful hosts and a guest is never made to feel conscious of the effort that has gone into a meal. For Thais, hospitality is a duty and an honour as well as a pleasure – "sanuk" in fact. Occasionally an honoured guest is treated to a "bassi"; prayers are recited around a structure of banana leaves forming an altar, which is crowned with an offering of flowers. After the religious ceremony, a narrow strip of white cotton is tied round the guest's wrist to symbolize his or her link with the hosts and with the spirits of the house. This is an old animist tradition whereby the cotton band is a protection against evil. It must not be cut, but left to fall off of its own accord. On feast days, the ancestors symbolically take part in the meal. Members of the family create a tasteful arrangement of flowers and desserts to place in front of the family spirit house. Care is taken to include as much yellow as possible, for this is the colour of Buddhism and good luck.

An old engraving of Thai ladies eating.

Old map of the Indochinese peninsula.

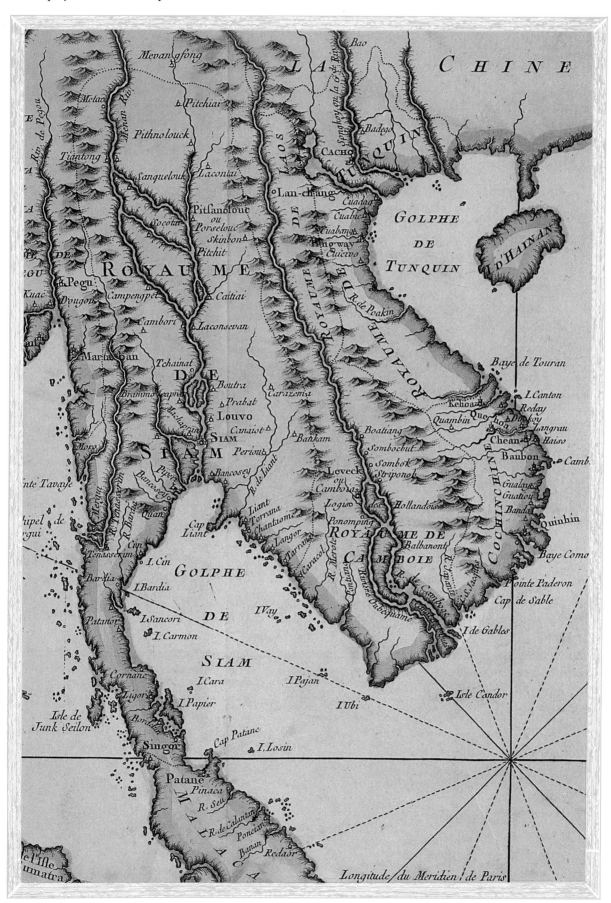

Chili Flowers

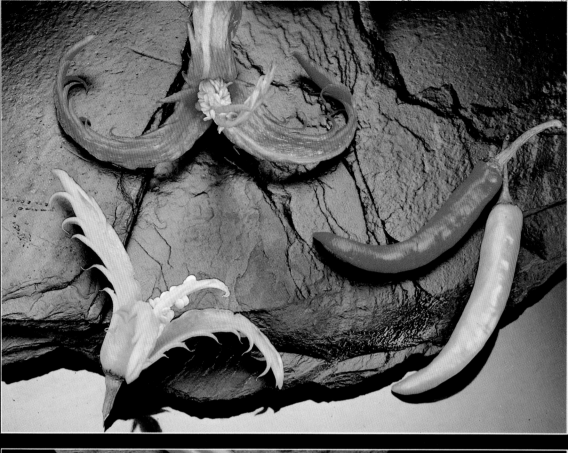

Tomato Baskets

Fruit and Vegetable Carving

Tomato Roses

Cucumber Lotuses

Fruit and Vegetable Carving

Thai cooks have developed their skills in cutting and carving to great advantage in the sculpting of vegetables and fruits into a multitude of forms. Pumpkins, turnips, tomatoes, carrots, cucumbers, radishes, chilies, onions and pineapples are transformed into roses, carnations, chrysanthemums, fish and animals.

King Rama II wrote a poem in which he told the story of a queen who had been banished from the palace by a rival. Disguised as a kitchen maid, she returned and managed to contact her son by carving scenes from her life on each piece of marrow for a marrow soup which he was to eat. Of course her son recognized them immediately and she was reinstated. Thus the tradition began.

The whole art of sculpting is too complex to describe in this book, but certain easy techniques have been chosen for you to experiment with.

SERVING A PINEAPPLE

Cut the top off the fruit (Figure 1).

Remove the skin, cutting thinly in order to retain the black spots on the fruit. Keep the stalk as a useful "handle" (Figure 2).

The black spots are in a spiral pattern round the fruit. Using a well-sharpened knife, score the fruit between the lines of spots. Two diagonal cuts will remove all the spots, leaving a spirally carved yellow pineapple (Figure 3).

Remove the stalk. Cut the pineapple lengthways into two, and then into four (Figure 4).

Remove the hard core from the centre of each quarter (Figure 5).

Reassemble the fruit using toothpicks to hold the slices together, and serve (Figure 6).

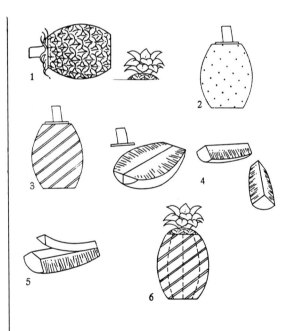

TOMATO BASKETS

Select smooth, firm tomatoes. Cut the top off each tomato to give a flat base (Figure 1).

Cut the tomato vertically and horizontally (Figures 2 and 3).

Carefully scoop out the pulp, leaving the basket (Figure 4).

If liked, the cutting can be done in a zigzag design to make the baskets more decorative.

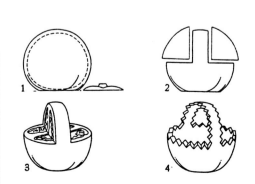

CHILI FLOWERS

Select smooth undamaged chilies of an even colour (Figure 1).

Using the point of a sharp knife, slit each chili several times lengthways, cutting from the base to the point (Figure 2). The cuts can be made to look spiky, for extra effect.

Toss the chilies into iced water. When the "flowers" open, remove the seeds (Figure 3).

TOMATO ROSES

Select smooth, firm tomatoes. Cut the top off each tomato (Figure 1).

Cut a very thin slice across the tomato at the same end, without cutting quite all the way through (Figure 2).

In a spiral motion remove the skin, together with a thin layer of the flesh underneath. The slice will become part of the spiral of skin (Figures 3 and 4).

When all the skin has been removed in one long strip, roll it up to form a rose, with the original slice forming the base (Figure 5).

CUCUMBER LOTUSES

Select small cucumbers. Cut off the ends, and then cut each cucumber in half (Figure 1).

With a small knife, trace eight equal triangles on the surface of the cut sections. Then continue each triangle down the length of the cucumber halves, cutting right to the centre but keeping them joined at the base (Figure 2).

Carefully shape the top of each triangle slice to resemble a petal (Figure 3).

Inserting the point of the knife as far as possible into the centre of the cucumber, cut the outline of the inside of each petal, following the dotted lines in the drawing (Figure 4).

Holding the cucumber together firmly, cut around it not more than 5 mm (¼ inch) in from the outside. Cut down as far as where the petals are joined at the base (Figure 5).

Repeat this cut another 5 mm (¼ inch) in (and a third time if the cucumber is large enough), scooping out the soft flesh in the centre.

Put the cucumber into iced water. The petals will open (Figure 6).

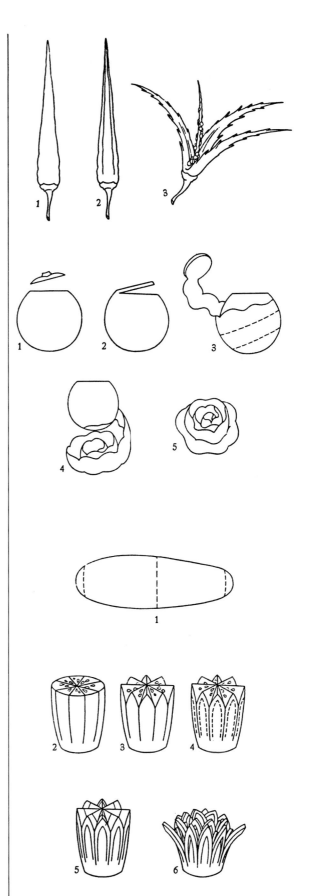

23

Ingredients

Spices, herbs and seasonings are inextricably linked with the history and food of Asia. Rhizomes, stalks, seeds or leaves, they should be used as fresh as possible to enjoy the rich flavours at their best. Some are available fresh in Asian shops around the world. Some, like basil, coriander and even chili or lemon grass can be cultivated under shelter in a garden or on a balcony. Others — turmeric, cardamom and galangal — may have to be purchased dried or in powder form. In this case the quantities given in these recipes should be halved.

Thai cooking depends very much on individual cooks varying the proportions of the different seasonings according to personal preferences. In this book a lot of the ingredients are measured by spoons in the traditional Thai way, with the deliberate intent of not being too precise. Occasionally certain ingredients, for example basil leaves, are given in only cup measures. This means that no exact amount is required — the cup is just a flexible guideline — and although an American measuring cup would be ideal, any medium-sized tea cup would do. This is rather like measuring rice by the handful — a very common habit in Asia. Where exact quantities are required, metric, Imperial and cup equivalents are given.

All the recipes serve 4-6 people although naturally this depends on how many other dishes are served at the same meal. We assume that rice and at least two other dishes will be served together.

Spicy dishes require less meat or fish than mild ones because extra rice is consumed with them to compensate for the spiciness.

BAMBOO SHOOTS *(Nor mai)*: The shoots of the bamboo are cut when they have grown about 15 cm (6 inches) above the ground. They need to be peeled and the inner, white part boiled for 30 minutes in water. However, the canned variety needs to be boiled for only 10 minutes and may be used immediately in soups or curries. Canned bamboo shoots, once opened, can be kept for up to a week in the fridge, if the water is renewed every day.

BASIL AND HOLY BASIL *(Horapha)*: Hindus believe that basil is sacred and they like to plant it in religious sanctuaries. The variety of basil they use is called holy basil and it has a spicy flavour. This is more difficult to find in the West than sweet basil, but pepper or finely chopped chili can be added to the sweet variety to compensate.

Both types of basil are used a lot in Thai cooking. Basil is also used for medicinal purposes, to treat indigestion and to stimulate the appetite.

BEANCURD *(Tao hou)*: This is a soya bean extract to which a setting agent has been added. Soft beancurd is white, and is used extensively in Chinese dishes. It is available in most oriental shops, and is usually sold in pieces 7.5 cm (3 inches) square. Hard, or dry, beancurd is made by compressing soft bean-curd. Beancurd is available in many other forms — fried, fermented, etc.

BEANSPROUTS *(Thua ngok)*: The sprouts of the soya or mung bean are crunchy and tender. They can be grown at home, but they are easy to find in most places nowadays. The canned variety are not a very good substitute but beansprouts can be replaced by other fresh vegetables, finely sliced, if necessary.

BERGAMOT *(Makroud)*: Also known as kaffir lime, this plant is found everywhere in Thailand and people often grow it at home.

The leaves have a delicate flavour, slightly lemony, which goes equally well with curries and seafood dishes. The fruit has a bumpy dark green rind with a concentration of aromatic oils and the aroma of lemon. Sometimes the juice of this fruit is used in Thai dishes instead of lime, or vice versa. The skin is also used in many Thai dishes, especially curries, and can be replaced by grated lime skin if necessary.

BURNT MILD CHILI PASTE: See Chili Pastes.

CARDAMOM *(Krawan)*: The queen of spices, cardamom has been used since ancient times. Produced mostly in India and Sri Lanka, it also grows in southeastern Thailand near Cambodia. Cardamom needs a humid climate to grow, and deforestation is endangering its survival. The aromatic pods can be green, white or black and they all contain a number of small seeds. The pods and seeds are used in different types of sweet or savoury Thai dishes, especially in curries.

Europeans have known Siamese cardamom since the 17th Century. It was one of the first spices exported to England, China and Japan.

Medicinally, cardamom can be used as a laxative and to relieve flatulence. In addition, cardamom is mixed with ginger and boiled, as a health drink.

Powdered cardamom is readily available but it is better to grind your own freshly if possible.

CELERY *(Khuen chai)*: Thai celery is much smaller than the variety found in the West. It is also greener, thinner-stemmed and more leafy, with a stronger celery flavour. However, either type can be used equally well for Thai soups, sautés and salads.

Young celery leaves make an attractive garnish which enhances the flavour of the food at the same time.

CHILIES *(Prik)*: Chauca, personal physician of Christopher Columbus, wrote that the Portuguese brought chilies from the West Indies to India and Africa in 1585.

The Thais add generous amounts of chilies to most of their dishes. No one region is known as the home of fiery food, as each province has its own "hot" dishes. Many different varieties of chili are used in Thailand but the most common is 7.5-10 cm (3-4 inches)

long and can be red, green or yellow when fresh. Dried, it is red. Another popular chili in Thai cooking is tiny, green and extremely fiery. The seeds are the hottest part of the chili so if you want to keep the flavour, without the heat, slit open the chilies and discard the seeds. Dried chilies should be soaked in hot water for 10 minutes before grinding. The Thai use chilis in almost every conceivable way — fresh, dried, whole, chopped, crushed or sliced into rings. Just a few words of caution, always wash your hands carefully after handling chilies and do not touch your eyes or mouth, or they will suffer from a burning sensation.

Apart from the flavour they impart, chilies are also good for the health. Followers of Thai traditional medicine believe that chilies help get rid of flatulence and stomach cramps. This is now thought to be because chilies can kill bacteria in the stomach and intestinal tract. Chili in the stomach produces increased levels of hydrochloric acid which, in turn, increases the blood circulation in the stomach lining. This helps to increase the rate of digestion. Blood pressure also rises as the heart beats faster. Thais also believe that those who sweat profusely after eating chilies are ridding themselves of toxic substances in the body.

CHILI PASTES *(Nam prik phao)*: These can be bought in bottles from Asian stores. A particularly popular one in Thai cooking, especially for seafood dishes, is burnt mild chili paste.

CHINESE MUSHROOMS *(Hed hom)*: These dried, whole mushrooms have a distinctive flavour. They should always be soaked in warm water for 30 minutes before being added to other ingredients. The stems are seldom eaten as they are quite tough.

Chinese mushrooms are extremely rich in calcium, phosphorus and potassium. Protein is especially high in dried mushrooms. Medicinally, Chinese mushrooms have been shown to reduce cholesterol levels in the blood. Some scientific research even suggests that these mushrooms have anti-viral and anti-tumour properties.

They are sold in most oriental food stores around the world.

CINNAMON *(Ob cheuy)*: In southern Asia, there are many varieties of cinnamon, the dried, aromatic bark of a member of the laurel

Greater galangal (top); ginger (centre); lesser galangal (left); tamarind pods.

family. In Thailand the "batavia" variety is commonly used to give a pleasant aroma to beef and chicken dishes.

Medicinally, Thais believe that it is an anti-acid and that it can reduce any overproduction of a nursing mother's milk.

Cinnamon can be found in powder form or in bark sticks. The bark retains its flavour for longer.

CLOVES *(Kan plou)*: Marco Polo thought that cloves came from Java, but Conti discovered that they actually orginated from the Moluccas Islands. From there the use of cloves spread to other parts of Southeast Asia and to Europe.

They are the dried flower buds of a member of the myrtle family and can be used whole or in powder form.

In Thai cuisine, cloves are added to curries and they also go very well with tomatoes, salty vegetables and ham. In Thailand, cloves have traditionally been chewed with betel leaves.

Medicinally, Thais believe that cloves kill bacteria and also act as an antispasmodic. Cloves can be chewed after meals, as some Thais do, to aid digestion.

COCONUT MILK AND CREAM *(Kathi)*: These two important ingredients are used in curries as well as in desserts and beverages. Coconut milk is the liquid squeezed from the grated flesh of mature coconut after the flesh has been soaked in lukewarm water. Coconut cream is a richer version. For coconut milk use 3 cups grated coconut to 5 cups water; for coconut cream use 3 cups coconut for 2½ cups water. Soak the coconut in the water for 15 minutes. Mix well with your hands, then tip into a muslin-lined strainer placed over a bowl. Squeeze all the liquid out of the muslin. The operation can be repeated with the already-squeezed coconut to produce thinner coconut milk which is acceptable in soups. All this is very time-consuming, and removing the flesh from a coconut is very difficult without the right implements. Luckily, ready-made coconut milk is available in cans in most places around the world. Stir the contents if coconut milk is required or scoop the cream off the top if you need coconut cream. Creamed coconut, frozen grated coconut and frozen coconut milk are also generally obtainable. However, if coconut is totally unavailable, then boiled milk may be used as a substitute.

Remember that coconut milk is not the liquid which is found inside a fresh young coconut. That water is only used in mixed tropical drinks, never in cooking, and has none of the properties of coconut milk.

CORIANDER *(Phakchee)*: This member of the carrot family has delicate leaves and deep roots. When the plant reaches maturity, it produces abundant white flowers. The leaves and seeds are used in many cuisines throughout the world, but Thai cooking makes use of the roots as well.

The round, beige seeds are added to curries and vegetables. The roots are crushed with garlic to flavour meat and are often added to

Coriander and mint leaves (top); bergamot fruit and leaves.

In a clockwise direction from the top: Chinese mushrooms; star anise; cinnamon; tamarind pulp; coriander seeds; small Thai garlic (centre).

soups, especially beef soups. The leaves are used extensively as a garnish.

CUMMIN *(Yira)*: Only the seeds are used, dried and ground. In Thai cuisine, cummin is used in sauces and on grilled meats. Cummin can be purchased already ground, but the whole seeds keep their flavour better and they are easy to grind at home.

DRIED LETTUCE LEAVES *(Tang chai)*: A fairly unusual ingredient in Thai cooking, this is sold in bottles in Asian stores.

DRIED SHRIMP *(Kung haeng)*: These are small salted shrimp dried in the sun. They are generally sold in powder form in bottles in most Asian stores.

FERMENTED SOYA BEANS *(Tao jiaw)*: Whole fermented yellow or black soya beans may be labelled "Dow See" in oriental stores. They are sold in bottles and the English label probably says "Yellow Bean Sauce". Fermented soya beans are nutritious, strongly flavoured and salty. They replace salt completely in some Thai dishes.

FISH SAUCE *(Nam pla)*: This thin, salty, pale brown sauce is made by filtering off the liquid from fermenting salted fish. Rich in the B vitamins and protein, it makes an excellent salt substitute. To be a good Thai cook, always have a bottle of fish sauce ready to add to Thai food.

As well as being used in cooking, it can be served as a sauce alone or mixed with lime and chili. You can use it and your imagination to create more elaborate sauces, as the Thais do.

Fish sauce is an exclusively Southeast Asian product. Thailand's superb sauce is well known and sold in Southeast Asian shops around the world.

GALANGAL *(Kha)*: Both greater and lesser galangal are related to ginger. In Thailand greater galangal is most commonly used; its aroma is subtler than that of lesser galangal and its inside is milky white. You often find it in curries and soups. It is used fresh in Asia, but elsewhere it may have to be purchased dried. In this case, soak the root in hot water for 1 hour before use and remove it before serving. Powdered galangal is also available.

Medicinally, galangal is classed as a digestive stimulant and Thais mix the grated root with lime juice to treat stomach ache. Thais also believe that galangal can help respiratory ailments.

GARLIC *(Krathiem)*: This member of the lily family is thought to originate from Asia. The Thai garlic head is made up of smaller cloves than the Western varieties. It is used abundantly in Thai cuisine.

Garlic contains significant amounts of vitamin C, calcium and protein. It is also rich in potassium, phosphorus, iron and zinc.

Medicinally, it is believed that garlic can reduce blood pressure and cleanse the blood of excess glucose. It is also said to alleviate 'flu, sore throats and bronchial congestion.

GINGER *(Khing)*: Native to India and China, ginger has been used medicinally for centuries. It was taken to Rome by caravans through Asia Minor. Ginger was probably one of the first Asian spices to reach Europe and it has been in use there since the Middle Ages.

The aromatic rhizome of the ginger plant is an important ingredient of Thai main dishes and desserts. It must be peeled before it can be chopped, grated or crushed. Fresh ginger is preferable, but powdered ginger can be substituted if necessary.

LEMON GRASS *(Takrai)*: This is one of the most common herbs in Thai food, It has long, lemony-smelling blades but only the lower part, which is white and bulbous, is used. It gives a unique flavour to curries and soups. A stalk of lemon grass is round and close packed like that of a very small leek.

Where fresh lemon grass is unavailable, dried stems (which should be removed before serving) or powdered lemon grass may be used. Also, thinly pared lemon peel is an acceptable substitute.

In traditional Thai medicine, lemon grass has long been used to treat colds and stomach aches. Also, it can be used to treat gallstones by drinking the water in which this herb has been boiled.

MINT *(Bai saranae)*: Leaves of the spearmint variety are often used in Thai salads, fish dishes and soups. Sweet basil leaves can be used as a substitute if necessary.

NOODLES: Chinese noodles may confuse you slightly to start with as there are so many different types made from different types of flour — mung bean, wheat or rice — and they come in a wide variety of shapes and sizes, sometimes fresh and sometimes dried. Fresh noodles can be found in some Asian shops outside Asia, but if not, packaged dried noodles can be used. These should be soaked in warm water before using but instructions are usually provided on the packet.

Bean thread vermicelli *(Woon sen)*: This type of noodle is made from mung beans. They are bought in long strands and are rather hard and semi-transparent, when uncooked. "Woon sen" are used in soups and some stir-fried dishes where they become transparent and gelatinous. They should be soaked in warm water before use unless they are to be deep fried, when they expand and become light and crisp like rice vermicelli.

Rice vermicelli *(Gwaytio sen mee)*: "Sen mee" are thin, brittle, semi-transparent noodles sold in dried form. They can be used directly from the packet if they are to be deep-fried. For use in soups or stir-fried dishes, they should be presoaked in warm water.

Rice noodles *(Gwaytio sen lek)*: "Sen lek" are very similar to "sen mee", but just a little wider and thicker.

Rice noodles *(Gwaytio sen yai)*: This is the only type of noodle which is packaged wet. Commonly used in soups and stir-fried dishes, the shape is much wider and slightly thicker than that of the "sen mee" and "sen lek" varieties.

Egg noodles *(Ba mee)*: These are made from wheat flour with the addition of egg. They are used in soups and stir-fried dishes. They come in different widths and some varieties are sold fresh, others only dried.

OYSTER SAUCE *(Nam man hoy)*: This delicious sauce is made from oysters blended with soya sauce and salt. It is sold in bottles and is traditionally served with sautéed vegetables.

PALM SUGAR *(Nam tarn puk)*: This tasty brown sugar is extracted from the sap of palm trees. It can be replaced by other brown sugars.

SESAME OIL *(Nam man nga)*: This concentrated, expensive oil is made from grilled sesame seeds and is used only in small quantities, mainly for flavouring. It is not the clear sesame oil sold in dietetic shops, and is available in most oriental food stores.

SHRIMP HEADS *(Hua kung)*: These are sold in bottles, mixed with oil, and are usually labelled "Shrimp Paste with Bean Oil".

SHRIMP PASTE *(Kapi)*: In former times, Thailand was an aquatic society. Water flowed near every household and in that water were many kinds of water crustacean, including shrimps. Perhaps this explains how "kapi", so beloved by the Thais, came about.

Shrimp paste, rich in the B vitamins, is also one of the main sources of protein in Southeast Asian diets. When visiting a Thai market, you can see several different kapi stands where shrimp pastes are sold in various forms and colours. The colours range from bright pink to dark brown, while the forms vary from soft and mushy to very dry and hard.

Shrimp paste has a very strong smell so it should either be purchased in small quantities or kept in an airtight container. It should always be fried or grilled before being eaten. It can be mixed with other ingredients or cooked on its own.

Thai kapi is exported everywhere around the world and is usually sold in small plastic containers. A recipe for home-made Shrimp Paste (Kapi) is on page 35.

SOYA SAUCE *(See iew)*: Made from soya beans, this is well known around the world. There are three main types used in Thai cooking. Be sure to select the appropriate one as they all taste very different. Light soya sauce is most frequently used and is thinner and lighter than the others. Dark soya sauce is black and thicker, with a stronger savoury flavour, and is used mainly in stews. Sweet soya sauce is thick, black and sweet.

They are all available in Chinese stores everywhere and keep almost indefinitely without refrigeration.

STAR ANISE *(Poy kak)*: An eight-pointed star-shaped seed pod from a relative of the magnolia, which is native to China. It has a strong aniseed flavour and European anise or fennel seeds can be substituted. However, star anise is sold in most Chinese provision stores and keeps well in an airtight container.

STICKY RICE *(Khao niaw)*: Also known as glutinous rice, it is available in short- and long-grain varieties. It has a rather cloudy appearance. When cooked it forms a sticky mass and is often used in desserts.

STRAW MUSHROOMS *(Hed fang)*: These globe-shaped mushrooms have a grey-black skin and are cream coloured inside. They are usually sold canned in water. Fresh straw mushrooms do not keep well.

TAMARIND *(Makham)*: The tamarind tree native to Asia has fernlike leaves and produces a bean-like fruit. Before it ripens, this pod is green and is eaten as a tasty tidbit. When ripe, the pod is brown and brittle on the outside, but the pulp inside is soft and juicy. This pulp is compressed and sold in packets. It adds an interesting tartness to many Thai dishes and is usually used in the form of tamarind juice. To make this, soak 1 tablespoon tamarind pulp in 4 tablespoons warm water for 5 minutes. Then squeeze and knead the tamarind to dissolve it, and strain out any seeds and fibre. Tamarind is widely available, sometimes dried, but can be replaced by lemon juice or a reduced quantity of vinegar as a last resort. Tamarind juice is a well-known laxative.

TURMERIC *(Khamin)*: Also called curcuma, this originates from Southeast Asia. The rhizome, which looks rather like ginger but is bright yellow inside, is crushed and fried with other curry ingredients to impart its colour to the dish. Ground or powdered turmeric is a satisfactory substitute if you cannot get the fresh or dried root. The shredded leaves are occasionally added to the cooking pot or used as a garnish.

The medicinal properties of turmeric are many since it is claimed that it can reduce muscular tension, treat diarrhoea, help regulate a woman's menstrual cycle and help prevent hepatitis and diseases of the eyes. Finally, in powder form mixed with palm oil, this root is said to be good for the skin.

Basics

Having introduced the ingredients of Thai cooking, we are now moving on to the "basics" of the cuisine. By this we mean recipes for items which are prepared in advance, to be used later in or with other dishes. The practice of having a bank of frequently used essentials is quite common in Asia — a kind of time-saving two-stage cuisine. Thai cooks would keep a constant stock of some of these basics; other items would be prepared specifically for a particular meal, but well before the rest of the dishes, ready to be incorporated or used as a garnish or accompaniment when required.

Khao Suoy

PLAIN RICE

Plain rice, cooked ahead but never overcooked, finds its way into a wide range of "khao phad" or fried rice dishes. It can be kept in the fridge for a day without becoming too flabby or stale.

3 cups uncooked rice gives 8-9 cups cooked rice.

3 cups (500 g/1 lb) long-grain rice

Wash the rice carefully and drain. Pour the rice into a medium saucepan and add enough water for the level to be 2.5 cm (1 inch) above the rice.

Bring to the boil and stir. Cover, leaving a small gap between the lid and the side of the pan. Cook over medium heat for 12-15 minutes.

When all the liquid has been absorbed, reduce heat and cook for a further 3 minutes.

Khao Man

COCONUT RICE

Coconut rice can be prepared with either ordinary or sticky rice, depending on what sort of dish it is to be served with. If using sticky rice, soak it first in plenty of water for at least 2 hours, but preferably overnight.

If prepared with ordinary rice, serve with Salted Sun-Dried Beef (Nua Dad Diao) or other savoury dishes. Sticky coconut rice is delicious with mangoes.

2 cups (350 g/12 oz) rice
2 cups (450 ml/¾ pint) water
1 cup (250 ml/8 fl oz) coconut cream
salt

Rinse and drain the rice and put into a pan with the water, coconut cream and salt. Mix well.

Bring to the boil over medium heat. Reduce the heat and cover. Simmer for 10 minutes.

When all the liquid has been absorbed, cook for a few more minutes over low heat. The resulting slight burning of the rice at the bottom of the pan gives extra flavour to this dish.

Mou Daeng

RED PORK

Red Pork is often purchased ready-prepared from Chinese delicatessen shops and markets but it can also be cooked at home. It is used in noodle dishes like Red Pork with Egg Noodles (Kuoy Tiaw Mou Daeng) or can be served as a simple meal with Plain Rice (Khao Suoy).

1 kg (2 lb) pork fillet
1 packet powdered red sauce
1 cup (250 ml/8 fl oz) water
2 tablespoons soya sauce (optional)

Garnish:
1 cucumber, sliced
coriander leaves

Cut the pork into long, thick slices. Dissolve the red sauce in the water, and add the soya sauce if desired.

Pour the sauce over the pork. Mix well and let the pork marinate for 1-2 hours. Arrange the slices in a roasting pan and cook in a hot oven (230°C/450°F/Gas Mark 8) for 30 minutes, turning the slices over once half way through.

Cut the slices into thin strips. Serve garnished with cucumber and coriander.

Red Pork

Nam Kaeng Jued

STOCK

Most Thai soups and some rice and noodle dishes use as a base, stock which has been prepared in advance. It can be kept in the refrigerator for a maximum of 3-4 days or in the freezer for long-term storage. This is a classic stock recipe, using one of three meats — chicken, pork or beef. If a vegetable stock is required simply omit the meat bones.

9 cups (2 litres/3½ pints) water
1 kg (2 lb) meat bones
2 cloves garlic
1 medium turnip
2 sticks celery
2 shallots
1 pinch ground ginger
ground black pepper

Bring all the ingredients to the boil in a large pan over medium heat.

Lower the heat and simmer for 1 hour. Strain.

Khai Jiew Han Foy

GARNISHING OMELETTE

This simple omelette can be used as a garnish for a wide variety of dishes.

1 tablespoon oil
1 egg, beaten

Heat the oil in a frying pan. Pour in the egg, and tilt the pan so that the egg covers the bottom. When the omelette is cooked, roll it up and slice into thin strips.

Ta Khay Khai

OMELETTE WEB

This can be tricky at first but the skill is easily learnt. It is a good idea to prepare some well in advance especially the first time you require them. They are not the sort of thing you should try out at the last minute before your guests arrive. 3 eggs will make about 5 webs.

3 eggs
oil

Break the eggs through a sieve into a bowl, breaking up the egg yolks with a fork. Do not beat them.

Heat a lightly oiled frying pan over low heat. Pour a little of the egg into the pan through a funnel, making the pattern of a spider's web or a net. Transfer carefully to a plate.

Krathiam Jiew

GOLDEN GARLIC

This makes a delicious seasoning in non-spicy soups and noodle dishes.

Sometimes the oil is not drained off and the garlic is served in the oil as a condiment or accompaniment with such dishes as Pork Tapioca Balls (Sakhou Sai Hou).

250 g (8 oz) garlic
1½ cups (350 ml/12 fl oz) oil

Coarsely chop the garlic. Heat the oil over medium heat, and add the garlic, stirring frequently.

When golden brown, remove from the heat, drain the garlic and leave to cool. Store in an airtight container. Once opened, Golden Garlic keeps for 1 week in the refrigerator.

Phak Dong

PICKLED VEGETABLES

Pickled vegetables are a popular accompaniment to meat, poultry and fish dishes in Thailand. They should be prepared at least 24 hours before serving.

½ cauliflower, split into florets
½ cucumber, sliced into thin rounds
3 carrots, sliced into rounds
3 slices fresh ginger
1 cup (250 ml/8 fl oz) water
½ cup (125 ml/4 fl oz) vinegar
1 cup (250 g/8 oz) sugar
1 tablespoon salt

Place the cauliflower, cucumber, carrots and ginger in a sterilized preserving jar.

Bring the water to the boil with the vinegar, sugar and salt. As soon as the mixture boils, stir and remove from the heat.

Allow the liquid to cool before pouring over the vegetables. Seal the jar.

Khai Khem

SALTED EGGS

These eggs are usually boiled or fried and served with Rice Soup (Khao Tom Kai). Once unsealed they will keep safely for 2-3 weeks in the brine at room temperature and even longer if refrigerated.

200 g (7 oz) salt
2 cups (450 ml/¾ pint) water
12 fresh eggs

Dissolve the salt in the water, and bring the solution to the boil. Leave to cool.

Place the eggs in a preserving jar and fill the jar with the salted water. Seal.

Keep for at least 15 days before eating.

Kapi

SHRIMP PASTE

This is an essential ingredient of innumerable Thai dishes.

shrimps
salt

Use only very small, whole, fresh shrimps. Wash them carefully, then mix with salt in the proportion of ⅔ shrimps to ⅓ salt by weight.

Leave to stand overnight. The next day, crush the shrimps in a mortar to form as fine a paste as possible. Shape into a small cake or cakes and leave to dry, preferably in the sun. Repeat this pounding and shaping the next day and the day after so as to make the paste extremely fine.

On the third day, put the paste into an airtight container and leave to mature for 2 months. The kapi can then be kept for years without refrigeration.

Khao Khua

GOLDEN RICE SEMOLINA

This is an essential ingredient of "larp" the spicy ground meat or fish dishes originally from the north.

2 tablespoons white rice

Grind the uncooked rice in a coffee grinder to form a fine rice semolina.

Heat a frying pan without adding any oil, and pour in the rice semolina. Stir with a wooden spoon until golden.

Sauces and Curry Pastes

"Nam" is the Thai word for water and "menam" means river. "Nam manao" is lemon juice and "nam som" is vinegar. "Nam oy" is sugar cane juice, "nam man" is oil and "nam man oy" is oyster sauce — excellent with sautéed vegetables. "Nam prik" indicates a thick, spicy sauce or curry paste and "nam wan" a syrup. But the most popular sauce in cooking, the queen of sauces, is "nam pla" or fish sauce. Made by fermenting salted fish in huge stone jars, then filtering off the liquid, it is often used instead of salt. A newcomer's nose may find it a little overpowering at first, but it would be sacrilege to substitute common-or-garden salt. The particular flavour of Thai cooking depends a lot on "nam pla" and the novice should adopt good "nam pla" habits from the start.

As well as being a key ingredient in many dishes, "nam pla" provides the base for most of the sauces served with them. When mixed with other ingredients, its aroma mingles with theirs and it ceases to stand out so strongly. Spicy, sweet and sour, savoury and sweet sauces can be made from it according to the other elements used. The commonest of these other ingredients are shrimp paste, tamarind, shallots, garlic, chilies and sugar. If certain items are difficult to find, substitute something more readily available which will achieve the same effect. For example lemon juice, green mangoes, cooking apples or grapefruit can be used to replace the sharp flavour imparted by tamarind.

It is best to make sauces at the last minute as the ingredients spoil if they marinate for too long. A blender can be used for mashing and mixing the soft ingredients, but the dry spices are much better ground with a pestle in a mortar. Sauces and pastes are served cold in bowls or saucers. For special occasions, tiny, individual sauce bowls are used, but at everyday family meals people dip their pieces of meat, fish or vegetable into a communal bowl. Alternatively, you can spoon a little sauce onto your own plate.

At a typical meal Thais have two or three different sauces. "Nam pla" mixed with lemon juice, shallots and chilies goes well with fish and seafood; "nam prik" — based on chili usually mixed with shrimp paste — is excellent with all vegetables whether they are raw, steamed, boiled or fried, and even when served with coconut cream. These "nam prik" curry pastes are also called for as an ingredient in many Thai dishes.

Following Chinese custom, soya sauce is served with certain snacks and with red pork. Soya sauce is made by marinating soya beans in salted water in the sun and then filtering the liquid. Although not as aromatic as "nam pla", its saltiness means that it can serve the same purpose, and when mixed with anchovy paste, it makes an acceptable substitute.

The following recipes will introduce you to the idea of Thai sauces and curry pastes but from this basic selection you will be able to invent your own. The number of variations achieved by combining the different flavours in varying proportions is infinite, and this flexibility and creativity is one of the essential characteristics of Thai cooking.

Sauce Nam Daeng

RED SAUCE

5 tablespoons tomato sauce (page 41)
1 tablespoon chili sauce (page 40)
1 tablespoon light soya sauce
1 teaspoon vinegar
1 teaspoon ground pepper
1 tablespoon sugar
1 tablespoon rice wine

Mix all the ingredients together in a bowl.

Nam Jim Sie Jew

VINEGAR AND SOYA SAUCE

6 tablespoons soya sauce
3 tablespoons vinegar
3 teaspoons caster sugar
3 cloves garlic, crushed
10 coriander leaves
1 small chili, sliced into rounds (optional)

Mix together the soya sauce, vinegar and sugar. Add the garlic, coriander and chili, if liked, and stir well. This sauce goes well with grilled meat and fish.

Nam Jim Carot

SWEET AND SOUR SAUCE WITH TURNIP AND CARROT

2 tablespoons vinegar
3 tablespoons sugar
3 teaspoons salt
3-4 tablespoons water
2 tablespoons finely grated turnip
2 tablespoons finely grated carrot
2 chilies, crushed

Bring to the boil the vinegar, sugar, salt and water. Pour the liquid into a bowl, and mix in the turnip, carrot and chilies. This sauce goes well with all the fried dishes.

Nam Jim Sateh

SATAY SAUCE

125 g (4 oz) preroasted peanuts
1 tablespoon coriander seeds
1 teaspoon cummin seeds
1 stalk lemon grass, finely chopped
3 slivers galangal, finely chopped
6 shallots, chopped
7 cloves garlic, chopped
3 dried chilies
1 teaspoon shrimp paste
1 tablespoon tomato sauce (page 41)
1 tablespoon sugar
1½ cups (350 ml/12 fl oz) coconut cream
2 tablespoons fish sauce

Grind the peanuts in a pestle and mortar, or a coffee grinder. Pound together the coriander seeds, cummin seeds, lemon grass, galangal, shallots, garlic, chilies, shrimp paste, tomato sauce and sugar to form a paste. Add the coconut cream and pound together.

Pour the mixture into a pan and bring to the boil. Add the peanuts and fish sauce. Mix well. Reduce the heat and simmer for 20 minutes to thicken the sauce.

This sauce is served in a small bowl with Chicken Satay (Sateh Kai).

Ajad

CUCUMBER SAUCE

6 tablespoons vinegar
4 tablespoons sugar
2 teaspoons salt
1 cup (250 ml/8 fl oz) water
½ cucumber, peeled and diced
8 tablespoons finely chopped shallots
1 small, fresh red chili, cut into fine rings
coriander leaves

Mix together the vinegar, sugar and salt with the water in a small pan. Bring to the boil and remove from the heat. Leave to cool. Add the cucumber, shallots and chili and sprinkle with coriander leaves.

Con Ham

COCONUT SAUCE WITH HAM

1 × 200 g (7 oz) slice cooked ham, diced
1 cup (250 ml/8 fl oz) coconut cream
½ cup (125 ml/4 fl oz) water
2 tablespoons natural yoghurt
2 teaspoons salt
pepper
½ tablespoon sugar
1 tablespoon vinegar or lemon juice
4 tablespoons chopped onion
½ green or red pepper (capsicum), sliced

Mix the ham, coconut cream, water and yoghurt in a pan, and bring to the boil.

Add the salt, pepper to taste, sugar and vinegar. Stir in the chopped onion and sliced pepper. Boil for 2 minutes before removing from the heat and serving with vegetables.

Nam Prik Khee Ka

CHILI SAUCE

3 shallots
1 large chili
4 cloves garlic
2 tablespoons fish sauce
1 tablespoon lemon juice
1 teaspoon sugar

The shallots, chili and garlic need to acquire a slightly burnt or smoky flavour for this sauce. Peel the outer skin off the shallots then place them with the chili and garlic under the grill, or in a hot oven (220°C/425°F/Gas Mark 7) or on foil over a flame or burner until the skins are slightly burnt.

Pound them together to form a thick paste. Stir in the fish sauce, lemon juice and sugar.

Serve with grilled fish.

Tao Jiaw Con

FERMENTED SOYA BEAN AND COCONUT SAUCE

½ cup (125 ml/4 fl oz) coconut cream
4 tablespoons water
½ cup (125 ml/4 fl oz) fermented soya beans
125 g (4 oz) shrimp or pork, minced or ground
2 tablespoons chopped shallots or onions
1 teaspoon fish sauce
1 teaspoon sugar
½ red pepper (capsicum), finely sliced
salt
vinegar
Garnish:
spring onions (scallions) or coriander leaves

Bring the coconut cream and water to the boil, and simmer for about 10 minutes until the mixture thickens.

Rinse and drain the soya beans, mash them to a creamy paste and pour into the coconut cream, stirring constantly to form a smooth sauce. Add the shrimp or pork and shallots and mix well. Simmer for a few minutes.

Add the fish sauce, sugar, red pepper, and salt and vinegar to taste. Stir well and cover. Cook for 2-3 minutes.

Serve in little dishes, sprinkling with chopped spring onion or coriander. This sauce goes very well with rice and vegetables.

Nam Pla Prik Kheenou

FISH SAUCE WITH SMALL CHILIES

2 tablespoons fish sauce
3 small chilies, sliced
½ shallot, sliced
2 tablespoons lemon juice

Mix all the ingredients together and serve in individual bowls, often as an accompaniment to Chicken Fried Rice (Khao Phad Kai) and Fried Rice with Chicken and Basil (Khao Phad Bai Horapha).

Coconut Cream Sauce (left): Shrimp Paste Sauce.

Nam Prik Kapi

SHRIMP PASTE SAUCE

1 tablespoon shrimp paste
1 tablespoon fish sauce
3 tablespoons lemon juice
1 tablespoon sugar
2 small chilies, finely chopped
2 cloves garlic, crushed

Place the shrimp paste on a piece of foil and cook it over a flame or burner for 1-2 minutes, or in a hot oven (220°C/425°F/Gas Mark 7) until the outside is slightly burnt.

Mix the fish sauce, lemon juice, sugar, chili and garlic in a bowl. Add the shrimp paste and mix well, adding a little hot water if the sauce is too thick.

Serve the sauce with raw or steamed vegetables, or grilled fish. Extra chilies and garlic can be added to the basic sauce if you want to make it hotter or more colourful.

Nam Jim Makhua Tet Phao

TOMATO SAUCE

2 large, ripe tomatoes
4 shallots
1 small chili
1 tablespoon fish sauce or soya sauce
salt
pepper

The tomatoes, shallots and chili need to acquire a slightly burnt or smoky flavour for this sauce. Peel the outer skin off the shallots but do not peel the tomatoes. Place the whole tomatoes, shallots and chili under the grill, or in a hot oven (220°C/425°F/Gas Mark 7) or on foil over a flame or burner until the skins are slightly burnt. Pound them together in a bowl. Stir in the fish sauce. Add salt and pepper to taste. Serve with grilled chicken.

Kathi Rad Phak Tom

COCONUT CREAM SAUCE

2 cups (450 ml/³⁄₄ pt) coconut cream
salt

Bring the coconut cream to the boil. Add a little salt and simmer over low heat, stirring continually, until it thickens. Serve with raw or steamed vegetables.

Nam Prik Makhua Tet

SPICY TOMATO SAUCE WITH MINCED PORK

2 small chilies
3 shallots
6 cloves garlic
1 stalk lemon grass, chopped
2 teaspoons salt
2 teaspoons shrimp paste
1 tablespoon chopped garlic
2 tablespoons oil
200 g (7 oz) pork, minced or ground
3 tomatoes, diced
3-4 tablespoons water
1-2 tablespoons fish sauce
1-2 teaspoons sugar

Pound together the chilies, shallots, garlic cloves, lemon grass and salt. Add the shrimp paste and mix thoroughly.

Sauté the chopped garlic in the oil, add the pounded ingredients and cook on low heat until the mixture turns golden.

Add the minced pork to the pan and sauté for 3-4 minutes. Add the tomatoes with the water. Increase the heat and bring to the boil. Pour in the fish sauce and sprinkle with sugar.

Serve in small bowls as an accompaniment to raw vegetables.

Nam Tao Jiaw

SOYA BEAN SAUCE

4 tablespoons canned soya beans
1 teaspoon dark soya sauce
1 tablespoon vinegar
1 teaspoon brown sugar
1 teaspoon crushed fresh ginger
1 red chili, cut into small rings

Drain the soya beans, retaining the juice. Pound the beans and then mix with their retained juice. Add all the other ingredients and mix well. This sauce goes well with Chicken Rice (Khao Man Kai).

Nam Prik Kaeng Daeng

RED CURRY PASTE

2 teaspoons cummin seeds
1 teaspoon coriander seeds
8 dried chilies
½ teaspoon finely chopped bergamot skin
1 teaspoon salt
1 teaspoon chopped lemon grass
2 tablespoons chopped shallots
1 tablespoon chopped garlic
1 tablespoon chopped galangal
1 tablespoon shrimp paste

Place the cummin and coriander seeds in a pan, without adding any oil. Dry-fry them, stirring, over medium heat for 1-2 minutes until they are slightly browned and give off a roasted aroma.

Coarsely chop the chilies and soak in water for 10 minutes. Drain. Pound all the ingredients together to produce a fine paste.

This curry paste goes well with all meats.

Nam Prik Kaeng Kari

YELLOW CURRY PASTE

1 teaspoon cummin seeds
1 teaspoon coriander seeds
8 dried chilies
½ teaspoon ground cinnamon
1 teaspoon salt
½ teaspoon ground cloves
1 tablespoon chopped lemon grass
2 tablespoons chopped shallots
1 tablespoon chopped garlic
1 tablespoon yellow curry powder

Place the cummin and coriander seeds in a pan without adding any oil. Dry-fry them, stirring, over medium heat for 1-2 minutes until they are slightly browned, and give off a roasted aroma.

Coarsely chop the chilies and soak in water for 10 minutes. Drain. Pound all the ingredients together to produce a fine paste which goes well with beef and pork.

Nam Prik Kaeng Khiew Wan

GREEN CURRY PASTE

1 teaspoon cummin seeds
1 teaspoon coriander seeds
6 fresh green chilies, chopped
1 tablespoon chopped lemon grass
1 teaspoon chopped coriander root
1 tablespoon chopped shallot
1 tablespoon chopped garlic
1 teaspoon chopped galangal
7 peppercorns
1 teaspoon salt
1 teaspoon shrimp paste

Place the cummin and coriander seeds in a pan, without adding any oil. Dry-fry them, stirring, over medium heat for 1-2 minutes until they are aromatic and slightly browned. Pound them with the remaining ingredients to produce a fine paste.

Nam Prik Kaeng Masaman

MASAMAN CURRY PASTE

10 dried red chilies
1 teaspoon cummin seeds
1 tablespoon coriander seeds
2 cardamom pods
3 cloves
6 tablespoons chopped garlic
4 tablespoons chopped shallots
1 tablespoon oil
10 peppercorns
2 tablespoons chopped lemon grass
1 teaspoon chopped galangal
1 teaspoon chopped bergamot skin
1 teaspoon chopped coriander root
1 teaspoon shrimp paste, grilled
1 cup (250 g/8 oz) palm sugar
1 tablespoon salt
4 tablespoons tamarind juice

Coarsely chop the chilies and soak in water for 10 minutes. Drain.

Dry-fry the cummin and coriander seeds, cardamom pods and cloves over medium heat for 1-2 minutes until they are aromatic and slightly browned.

Sauté the chilies, garlic and shallots in the oil until lightly browned.

Pound the spices in the following order:
a) garlic, shallots and chilies
b) coriander, cardamom pods, cummin, cloves and peppercorns
c) lemon grass, galangal, bergamot, coriander roots

Place the shrimp paste on a piece of foil and cook it over a flame or burner for 1-2 minutes, or in a hot oven (220°C/425°F/Gas Mark 7) until the outside is slightly burnt. Mix the shrimp paste with all the above ingredients plus the sugar, salt and tamarind juice to form a fine paste.

Nam Prik Kaeng Som

SOUR CURRY PASTE

10 dried chilies
5 shallots, chopped
1 tablespoon shrimp paste
1 tablespoon salt

Coarsely chop the chilies and soak in water for 10 minutes. Drain. Pound all the ingredients together to produce a coarse paste which goes well with fish and vegetables.

Nam Prik Kaeng Phanang

PHANANG CURRY PASTE

9 large dried red chilies
7 shallots, chopped
6 cloves garlic
2 teaspoons chopped coriander roots
15 peppercorns
3 slivers galangal
2 stalks lemon grass, chopped
1 tablespoon coriander seeds
1 tablespoon cummin seeds
1 teaspoon shrimp paste
1 teaspoon salt

Coarsely chop the chilies and soak in water for 10 minutes. Drain. Pound together all the ingredients to produce a fine paste.

Rice and Noodles

The Thais have cultivated rice since the earliest days of their history and although Thailand contains many jewels, to the Thais no gem can rival the pearly white rice which is produced in abundance and which has staved off famine throughout Thai history. It is their staff of life, their yardstick by which well-being is measured. A Thai will not ask, "Have you had lunch?" but "Have you eaten rice?"

In May they go to the fields to weed and clean in preparation for the ploughing. As soon as the first rains fall, usually in May, they sow the rice. The shoots grow quickly in the monsoon, and then the young plants are removed from the nursery to be replanted in the fields. Harvesting is in January. The government has now set up an efficient irrigation network which gives a second harvest in some areas. The rice is threshed on the spot in the fields, the straw and roots being burned to improve the soil.

The Rice-Planting Festival or Ploughing Ceremony takes place in May on an auspicious day designated by the Royal Astrologer. A court official, selected by the King, presides over the ceremony in which a symbolic furrow is made by a golden plough pulled by oxen on the green expanse of the Sanam Luang (Royal Field) in Bangkok. Specially blessed rice seeds are thrown into the furrow. Then, different foods are offered to the oxen. According to the food they choose, the Brahman priests, who still have an important place in Thai religious and ceremonial life, are able to predict the coming year's harvest.

Among the many varieties of rice, Thailand boasts a particularly fine, long-grain type which is generally destined for export. In Thailand, people eat white rice, without the husk. They cook it in water without salt to balance the spiciness of the accompanying dishes. A charcoal burner and aluminium pan are all the equipment they need. The secret of perfect rice-cooking lies in the quantity of water used; the level of water in the pan should be at one knuckle above the rice. All the water should be absorbed during cooking, leaving the rice firm and fluffy. Glutinous rice is a speciality of the hill people, and of the Issans who live in the northeast, but otherwise is generally used in desserts.

Thais usually cook more rice than is necessary for one meal. The remainder is used in a wide variety of "khao phad" (fried rice) dishes, mixing it with chicken, ham, prawns (shrimp), eggs, etc and flavouring it with garlic, onion and basil. The ingredients can be chopped, sliced, ground or crushed before being mixed with the rice and then fried. The best utensil for frying rice is a wok (a deep, conical pan) which can easily be obtained in oriental shops. Strong heat is needed and the rice must be stirred vigorously. This can lead to splashes and penetrating smells. In Thailand, the kitchen is sensibly located in a small, open-sided wooden outhouse, and the breeze carries away strong smells. In the West an efficient extractor fan in the kitchen would be a suitable alternative. "Khao phad" makes a meal on its own, whilst plain rice is served with a selection of meat, fish and vegetable dishes.

Thailand, like other Asian countries similarly influenced by the Chinese, has many noodle dishes using a wide variety of types of noodles. Mung bean noodles, rice noodles and wheat flour noodles, with or without egg, all find their way into delicious recipes cooked in various ways and combined with different ingredients.

Khao Phad Mou Ham

HAM FRIED RICE

2 cloves garlic, crushed
2 tablespoons oil
2 thick slices cooked ham, diced
4 cups (750 g/1½ lb) cooked plain rice (page 32)
4 tablespoons frozen peas, cooked
1 tablespoon soya sauce
pepper
1 egg, beaten
Garnish:
1 cucumber, sliced into rounds
6 spring onions (scallions)

Brown the garlic in the oil. Add the ham and sauté for a few minutes.

Turn up the heat. Add the rice and continue to sauté. Stir in the peas, soya sauce and pepper.

Remove half the mixture from the pan. Pour the egg into the empty half of the pan, and mix well with the rice preparation. Add the rest of the mixture and stir well together.

Serve in a large dish, garnished with cucumber rounds and spring onions.

Khao Phad Kapi

FRIED RICE WITH SHRIMP PASTE

2 tablespoons shrimp paste
2 tablespoons water
4 cups (750 g/1½ lb) cooked plain rice (page 32)
2 cloves garlic, crushed
3 tablespoons oil
salt
2 tablespoons dried shrimp
Garnish:
4 shallots, finely sliced
¼ red pepper (capsicum), cut into strips
garnishing omelette using 2 eggs (page 34)
lemon quarters

Dilute the shrimp paste in the water, then mix it well with the rice.

In a large pan brown the garlic in the oil. Add the rice and sauté over medium heat for 5 minutes, adding salt to taste. Reduce the dried shrimp to a powder in a blender. Sprinkle the powdered dried shrimp over the rice. Remove from the heat.

Serve in a large serving dish garnished with the shallot, strips of red pepper and thin slices of omelette. Add the lemon quarters.

Khao Phad Khi Mao

CHILI FRIED RICE

3 cloves garlic
1 teaspoon salt
4 shallots, chopped
4 small fresh red chilies
125 g (4 oz) beef fillet, minced or ground
1 tablespoon fish sauce
1 tablespoon soya sauce
1 teaspoon sugar
15 French beans, cut into small pieces
2 tablespoons oil
1 small can red kidney beans, drained
4 tablespoons fresh or frozen peas, cooked
1 cup basil leaves
4 cups (750 g/1½ lb) cooked plain rice (page 32)
freshly ground black pepper

Pound together the garlic, salt, shallots and chilies to form a paste.

Mix the beef with the fish sauce, soya sauce, sugar and French beans.

Heat the oil in a large pan and cook the paste made from chilies and shallots for 1-2 minutes. Add the meat mixture. Brown, stirring continuously. Add the red kidney beans and the peas. Cook for a moment whilst mixing.

Add the basil leaves and stir. Add the rice, and sauté over strong heat, adding pepper to taste.

Khao Phad Kai

CHICKEN FRIED RICE

1 tablespoon chopped garlic
3 tablespoons oil
1 tablespoon chopped onion
300 g (10 oz) chicken, diced
4 cups (750 g/1½ lb) cooked plain rice (page 32)
2 tablespoons fish sauce
1 teaspoon ground white pepper
2 eggs, beaten
Garnish:
1 cucumber, sliced into rounds
6 spring onions (scallions)
1 lime
1 teaspoon chopped coriander leaves

Brown the garlic in the oil. Add the onion, then add the chicken and stir-fry.

Add the rice and continue to stir-fry over strong heat. Add the fish sauce and pepper.

Make a hole in the centre of the rice mixture and pour in the egg. Stir well with a wooden spoon until the egg is cooked.

Serve, garnished with cucumber rounds, spring onions and slices of lime. Sprinkle with coriander.

This dish should be accompanied by Fish Sauce with Small Chilies (Nam Pla Prik Kheenon) served in small individual dishes.

Khao Phad Thalay Khi Mao

SPICY FRIED RICE WITH MIXED SEAFOOD

300 g (10 oz) seafood (e.g. squid, shelled prawns/shrimp, fish meat, crab meat)
3 cloves garlic
4 shallots
4 small red chilies
1 tablespoon salt
3 tablespoons oil
4 cups (750 g/1½ lb) cooked plain rice (page 32)
1 teaspoon sugar
1 tablespoon soya sauce
1 tablespoon fish sauce
1 cup basil leaves
Garnish:
3 chilies

Cut the seafood into bite-sized pieces. Throw it into boiling water for 3 minutes, drain and put aside.

Pound the garlic, shallots, chilies and salt together to produce a paste. Brown this paste in the hot oil and then sauté the rice in it.

Add the reserved seafood and mix well over strong heat. Add the sugar, soya sauce, fish sauce and basil leaves. Stir well and cook for a minute.

Serve hot, garnished with whole chilies. To make this dish particularly attractive you can mix only half the basil leaves in with the rice, sautéing the other half separately and arranging around the edge as a garnish.

Spicy Fried Rice with Mixed Seafood

Fried Rice with Chicken and Basil

Khao Phad Bai Horapha

FRIED RICE WITH CHICKEN AND BASIL

2 cloves garlic, crushed
2 small chilies, crushed
4 tablespoons oil
300 g (10 oz) chicken breast, finely sliced
2 tablespoons fish sauce
20 basil leaves
4 cups (750 g/1½ lb) cooked plain rice (page 32)
Garnish:
1 shallot, chopped and fried in a little oil

In a large pan lightly brown the garlic and chili in the oil. Add the chicken and sauté for 2-3 minutes before mixing in the fish sauce and the basil leaves. Take out a few basil leaves for garnish before adding the rice. Sauté over strong heat for 3 minutes, stirring briskly. Remove from the heat.

Transfer to a large serving dish or individual bowls. Garnish with the reserved basil leaves and the fried shallot.

Serve with Fish Sauce with Small Chilies (Nam Pla Prik Kheenon).

Khao Phad Man Kung

SHRIMP HEAD FRIED RICE

300 g (10 oz) small prawns (shrimp)
2 cloves garlic, crushed
4 tablespoons oil
1 tablespoon bottled shrimp heads
4-5 shallots, chopped
2 tablespoons fish sauce
salt
4 cups (750 g/1½ lb) cooked plain rice (page 32)
Garnish:
6 spring onions (scallions)
1 cucumber, sliced
coriander leaves

Shell and clean the prawns. Brown the garlic in the oil then add the shrimp heads, shallots and fish sauce. Add salt to taste and stir well.

Stir in the prawns and sauté for 1 minute. Add the rice, and sauté for a further 3 minutes.

Serve in a large dish, garnished with spring onions, cucumber rounds and coriander leaves.

Khao Phad Sam Si

THREE COLOURS FRIED RICE

2 cloves garlic, crushed
3 tablespoons oil
300 g (10 oz) pork, cut into thin strips
125 g (4 oz) blanched almonds
3 tablespoons fish sauce
4 cups (750 g/1½ lb) cooked plain rice (page 32)
1 large tomato, diced
250 g (8 oz) fresh or frozen peas, cooked
pepper
To serve:
lemon quarters

In a large pan lightly brown the garlic in the oil. Add the pork and almonds, and sauté for 3-4 minutes. Add the fish sauce. Cook for a further few minutes until the meat is cooked. Add the rice and turn up the heat, stirring well. Mix in the tomato. Cook for 2 minutes. Stir in the peas. Add pepper to taste.

Serve hot in a large serving dish with the lemon quarters.

Khao Man Kai

CHICKEN RICE

4 chicken breasts
3 cups (750 ml/1¼ pints) water
4 chicken bones
2 coriander roots
1 teaspoon salt
2 cups (400 g/14 oz) uncooked rice
4 tablespoons oil
6 cloves garlic, lightly crushed
Garnish:
coriander leaves
3 small cucumbers, sliced

Simmer the chicken in the water, with the bones, coriander roots and salt for 15-20 minutes. Skim off the froth and remove the chicken. Strain and reserve the stock.

Rinse and drain the rice. Heat the oil in a frying pan or wok and lightly brown the garlic. Add the rice to the garlic and cook for 3-4 minutes, stirring a little to prevent it from sticking.

Transfer the rice to a saucepan and add the strained chicken stock. Half cover the pan and boil until all the water has been absorbed. Lower the heat and cook for a few more minutes to dry the rice.

Slice the drained chicken breasts. Pile the rice onto a serving dish. Arrange the chicken slices on top and garnish with coriander leaves and slices of cucumber.

Khao Phad Mou

PORK FRIED RICE WITH TOMATO SAUCE

3 cloves garlic, crushed
2 tablespoons oil
300 g (10 oz) chicken or pork, finely sliced
1 onion, diced
2 tablespoons fish sauce or soya sauce
3 tablespoons canned tomato purée
4 cups (750 g/1½ lb) cooked plain rice (page 32)
pepper
Garnish:
1 cucumber, sliced into rounds
4 spring onions (scallions)
coriander leaves (optional)
1 lemon (optional)

Brown the garlic in the oil. Add the chicken or pork and sauté for about 3 minutes.

Add the onion, fish sauce and tomato purée. Stir well, adding a little water and oil if the mixture becomes too dry.

Turn up the heat. When the mixture is cooked after about 3 minutes more, add the rice and sauté for a further 3 minutes. Season to taste with pepper.

Serve in a large dish, garnished with cucumber rounds and spring onions. If desired, sprinkle with coriander leaves and squeeze lemon juice over the rice if you like it sour.

Khao Phad Broccoli

FRIED RICE WITH BROCCOLI AND MEAT

125 g (4 oz) small prawns (shrimp)
2 cloves garlic, crushed
1 tablespoon oil
125 g (4 oz) chicken, finely sliced
1 × 250 g (8 oz) broccoli, sliced
1 small carrot, finely sliced in rings
salt
1 tablespoon soya sauce
pepper
4 cups (750 g/1½ lb) cooked plain rice (page 32)

Shell the prawns. Brown the garlic in the oil, then add the chicken and sauté over strong heat.

When the chicken begins to cook, add the broccoli and carrot. Add salt to taste. Reduce the heat, stir well and allow to cook gently for 2-3 minutes.

Add the prawns and soya sauce. Season with pepper, and stir well.

Increase the heat. When the mixture is cooked and the prawns have turned pink, add the rice and sauté for a further 3 minutes.

Khao Phad Kari

CURRY FRIED RICE

2 shallots, sliced
1 tablespoon oil
1 onion, sliced
75 g (3 oz) butter
1 teaspoon curry powder
4 cups (750 g/1½ lb) cooked plain rice (page 32)
2 tablespoons raisins
salt
pepper

In a large pan brown the shallots in the oil. Add the onion and the butter. When the onion turns golden brown stir in the curry powder.

Increase the heat, add the rice, and sauté for a few minutes. Stir in the raisins, salt and pepper. Remove from the heat. Serve hot.

Pineapple Rice

Spicy Fried Noodles with Seafood

Khao Phad Sapparod

PINEAPPLE RICE

1 pineapple
300 g (10 oz) chicken breast
1 × 150 g (5 oz) slice ham
3 shallots, chopped (optional)
2 tablespoons oil
4 cups (750 g/1½ lb) cooked plain rice (page 32)
1 tablespoon soya sauce
pepper
Garnish:
coriander leaves
1 red pepper (capsicum), cut into strips
2 slices cucumber

Cut the pineapple in two, lengthways. Scoop out the fruit.

Dice enough of the fruit to fill a cup. Reserve the outside shells. Dice the chicken and ham.

Brown the shallots, if using, in the oil. Remove from the pan and put aside.

Sauté the diced chicken in the same oil. Add the rice and stir well.

Add the ham and soya sauce. Stir and add the diced pineapple. Season with pepper. Mix well and remove from the heat.

Gently heat the pineapple shells in a moderate oven (160°C, 325°F, Gas Mark 3) for 10 minutes and then fill with the rice mixture.

The pineapple can then be sprinkled with the fried shallots mixed with coriander leaves and strips of red pepper, or garnished with cucumber slices.

Kuoy Tiaw Phad See Iew

FRIED NOODLES WITH SOYA SAUCE

1 cup (250 ml/8 fl oz) oil
500 g (1 lb) rice vermicelli (sen mee)
2 tablespoons dark soya sauce
2 tablespoons crushed garlic
300 g (10 oz) broccoli, sliced
350 g (12 oz) fillet beef, diced
1 tablespoon light soya sauce
salt and pepper

Heat half the oil in a large frying pan. Sauté the vermicelli noodles in it, over strong heat for 2-3 minutes. Drain, add the dark soya sauce, mix well, and put to one side.

Heat the remaining oil over medium heat, and brown the garlic. Sauté the broccoli in the garlic oil then stir in the beef and light soya sauce. Cook for about 3 minutes, then mix the noodles with the meat and broccoli. Season with salt and pepper to taste.

Kuoy Tiaw Phad Khi Mao Thalay

SPICY FRIED NOODLES WITH SEAFOOD

500 g (1 lb) seafood (e.g. squid, shelled prawns/shrimp, fish meat, steamed mussels)
3 tablespoons crushed garlic
10 tablespoons oil
2 tablespoons soya sauce
500 g (1 lb) thick rice noodles (sen yai)
3 tablespoons fish sauce
a few holy basil leaves
3 chilies, roughly chopped
pepper

Cut the seafood into pieces if necessary. For instructions on steaming mussels, see page 74.

Brown the garlic in 4 tablespoons oil. Sauté the seafood for a few minutes in the same oil. Drain and put to one side.

Add the rest of the oil to the pan and increase the heat. Add the soya sauce and noodles and sauté for 2-3 minutes. Add the cooked seafood and the fish sauce. Stir well. Add the basil leaves and chilies and stir. Add pepper to taste and cook for a minute more.

Macaroni Phad

THAI MACARONI

250 g (8 oz) macaroni
salt
200 g (7 oz) shelled prawns (shrimp)
3 spring onions (scallions)
3 onions, chopped
2 tablespoons oil
1 tomato, diced
2 tablespoons tomato purée
2 tablespoons Maggi sauce
1 tablespoon soya sauce
pepper
grated cheese (optional)

Cook the macaroni in boiling, salted water for about 15 minutes or until *al dente*. Drain.

Cut the prawns down their backs to flatten them. Cut the spring onions into 2.5-cm (1-inch) lengths.

Brown the onions lightly in the oil. Add the tomato, tomato purée, Maggi sauce and soya sauce, and stir well. Cover and cook for 2 minutes.

Add the prawns and stir-fry for 2 minutes. Mix the prawn mixture with the macaroni and spring onions. Season with pepper.

Serve hot. Grated cheese can be sprinkled over this dish, if liked.

Rad Na Nua Sab

NOODLES WITH MEAT SAUCE

500 g (1 lb) egg noodles
6 lettuce leaves
1 teaspoon chopped garlic
10 tablespoons oil
½ tablespoon dark soya sauce
2 tablespoons chopped shallot
400 g (14 oz) beef, minced or ground
½ cup (125 ml/4 fl oz) water.
1 teaspoon curry powder
3 tablespoons light soya sauce
½ teaspoon flour, blended with
2 tablespoons water
salt and pepper

Garnish:
1 tablespoon chopped celery

Cook the noodles in boiling water according to the instructions on the packet. Drain. Line a salad bowl with the lettuce leaves.

Brown the garlic in 6 tablespoons oil. Sauté the noodles in this mixture for 1-2 minutes, adding the dark soya sauce. Pour the noodles over the lettuce leaves.

Brown the shallot in the rest of the oil. Add the meat, water, curry powder and light soya sauce, and stir well. When the sauce begins to boil, stir in the blended flour and add salt and pepper to taste. Simmer for a few minutes, before pouring the mixture over the noodles.

Just before serving, sprinkle with the celery.

Kuoy Tiaw Mou Daeng

RED PORK WITH EGG NOODLES

2 tablespoons chopped garlic
3 tablespoons oil
300 g (10 oz) egg noodles
1 tablespoon fish sauce
½ tablespoon dried lettuce leaves
1 cup beansprouts
300 g (10 oz) red pork (page 33)
pepper
Garnish:
1 tablespoon coriander leaves

Brown the garlic in the oil, and put the mixture to one side.

Cook the noodles according to the instructions on the packet. Drain, and place in a large bowl.

Stir the garlic and oil, fish sauce and lettuce into the noodles.

Poach the beansprouts in simmering water for 1 minute. Drain, and place in individual bowls.

Place the noodle mixture on top of the bean sprouts.

Arrange the thin strips of pork on the noodles. Season with pepper, and sprinkle with coriander leaves.

Soups

In Thai markets, the china stalls display far fewer plates than bowls. This is not surprising as bowls are much more appropriate for the two most popular dishes, rice and soup. Soup is eaten from dawn to dusk, on land and water. Pavements are crowded with soup stalls, soup-vending boats paddle up and down the "klongs" (canals) and bicycles adapted for easy soup-making patrol the "sois" (lanes). From a simple rice stock flavoured with soya sauce to gourmet extravaganzas with bergamot, lemon grass, lime juice and chilies, the aromas of soups contribute a special part of everyday Thai life.

There are three main types of soups. The first is that royal soup, the "tom yam", the most famous version of which, "tom yam kung", is made with prawns. It usually arrives in a charcoal-heated steamboat which takes pride of place on the table. This is a copper pot with a chimney, and underneath there is a place for red-hot charcoal. If you happen to possess one, now is the time to impress your guests with it. The soup continues to cook in the bowl surrounding the chimney during the meal. As the large pink prawns are fished out and savoured, the soup reduces, producing a delicious liquid redolent of lemon grass and fresh chilies. Tom yams can also be made with pork, chicken or mixed seafood. This gastronomic masterpiece relies on a combination of lemon juice, galangal, lemon grass, bergamot and chili to produce its inimitable flavour. The quantity of chili can be modified according to taste, but it does not take long to get used to that mixture of fire and freshness. It is a pity to do without it altogether; some marriages are indissoluble!

In contrast, "kaeng jued" is a mild Chinese soup, rather like a consommé, with meat and vegetables. As it is gentle on the palate, it makes a pleasant accompaniment to spicier dishes. The Thais sometimes add their own flavour to it by using coriander root.

"Khao tom", a clear rice soup, is a sort of universal healer. It is a favourite "morning after" remedy following an alcoholic evening, and also soothes stomach upsets, fevers, colds and anything else that entails feeling out-of-sorts. The rice is well cooked in a large quantity of water. Before serving, it can be seasoned with "nam pla", vinegar or chilies according to taste, and augmented with some meat or poultry.

It seems strange that hot soups should be so satisfying in such a hot country but a great deal of pleasure is gained from sitting around a steaming bowl from which each person serves him or herself, sharing togetherness with the soup. Soups are often served throughout a meal but they can, of course, constitute a meal in themselves, containing meat or fish and vegetables, and eaten with rice or noodles.

The base of most Thai soups is a chicken or pork stock, made in advance and put to one side. In the West, the variety of packaged stocks makes soup a very easy dish to prepare.

It is said that the original Chinese immigrants to Thailand had scarcely more than a little rice to put in their soup. In order to give some flavour to their meal they sucked pebbles dipped in fish sauce. We hope your Thai soup will be less austere!

Thalay Tom Klong

SEAFOOD SOUP

1 stalk lemon grass
4 cups (1 litre/1¾ pints) water
10 slivers galangal
4 tablespoons lemon juice
5 bergamot leaves
3 teaspoons salt
200 g (7 oz) fish fillets, finely sliced
200 g (7 oz) prawns (shrimp), shelled
12 oysters
125 g (4 oz) squid, finely sliced
1 fish head (optional)

Cut the lemon grass into 2.5-cm (1-inch) pieces. Bring the water to the boil. When boiling, add the galangal, lemon grass, lemon juice, bergamot and salt.

Return to the boil, and add the fish and seafood. Cook for a few minutes then remove from the heat and serve.

Alternatively, this soup can be cooked at the table, like a fondue. Heat the water and seasonings in a Chinese steamboat or a pan on a burner or hot plate. Arrange the fish and seafood in individual dishes for each diner to cook his own in the stock. It is best to serve the oysters on ice.

Tom Jued Hed

MUSHROOM SOUP

4 cups (1 litre/1¾ pints) water
3 shallots, chopped
2 tablespoons fish sauce
700 g (1½ lb) straw mushrooms, chopped
pepper

Bring the water to the boil and add the shallots and fish sauce. Continue to boil for 2-3 minutes.

Add the mushrooms and simmer for 5 minutes, half covering the pan.

Add pepper to taste before serving.

Tom Klong Kung

PRAWN AND TAMARIND SOUP

pulp of 2 tamarinds
4 cups (1 litre/1¾ pints) chicken stock (page 34)
salt
2 shallots, crushed
10 prawns (shrimp), shelled
1 tablespoon lemon juice
2 small green chilies

Crush the tamarind pulp in a little water then heat the stock with the strained tamarind liquid and salt to taste.

Crush the shallots in a mortar and add to the stock.

When it begins to boil, add the prawns. Cook for about 2 minutes. When the prawns turn pink, the soup is ready.

Before serving, add the lemon juice and the whole chilies.

Khao Tom Kai

RICE SOUP

4 cups (1 litre/1¾ pints) water
½ cup (75 g/3 oz) rice
250 g (8 oz) pork or chicken, minced or ground
2 tablespoons fish sauce
1 pinch celery salt
1 pinch pepper
Garnish:
1 tablespoon chopped coriander and
spring onion (scallion)

Bring the water to the boil, add the rice and cook for 20 minutes.

Add the meat, fish sauce, celery, salt and pepper. Cook for 5 minutes.

Serve in individual bowls sprinkling each one with a little of the mixed coriander and spring onion.

Stuffed Cucumber Soup

Chicken Soup with Galangal

Kaeng Jued Tang Kwa Sord Sai

STUFFED CUCUMBER SOUP

4 small cucumbers
1 coriander or parsley root
5 cloves garlic
pepper
300 g (10 oz) pork, minced or ground
1 teaspoon light soya sauce
4 cups (1 litre/1¾ pints) pork stock (page 34)
Garnish:
coriander leaves

Cut both ends off each of the washed cucumbers. Scrape out the flesh and discard.

Pound the coriander root, garlic and pepper. Mix this mixture with the pork and soya sauce and knead together.

Fill the cucumbers with this stuffing. Cut into slices at least 2.5 cm (1 inch) thick. Push a toothpick crossways through each slice to prevent the stuffing from falling out.

Heat the stock. When hot, add the stuffed cucumber slices. Cover, and simmer for 10 minutes. Garnish with coriander leaves. If preferred, the stuffed cucumbers can be simmered while still whole, and sliced before serving.

Kai Tom Kha

CHICKEN SOUP WITH GALANGAL

2 stalks lemon grass
1 cup (250 ml/8 fl oz) water
4 cups (1 litre/1¾ pints) coconut milk
8 chicken thighs or
600 g (1¼ lb) chicken breast, diced
10 slivers galangal
2 tablespoons fish sauce
3 small fresh chilies
3 bergamot leaves
2 tablespoons lemon juice
Garnish:
spring onions (scallions) and chilies, shredded

Cut the lemon grass into 2.5-cm (1-inch) pieces. Bring the water to the boil with half the coconut milk. Then add the chicken, lemon grass, galangal and 1 tablespoon fish sauce. Simmer for about 20 minutes or until the chicken is cooked. Less cooking time will be required for diced chicken breast.

Stir in the remaining coconut milk and turn up the heat. As soon as it begins to boil, toss in the whole chilies and bergamot leaves. Stir, and remove from the heat.

Serve in individual bowls. Sprinkle each with lemon juice and fish sauce to taste and garnish with slivers of spring onion and chili.

Tom Yam Pla Chon

FISH SOUP

2 stalks lemon grass
2 cloves garlic
3 shallots
1 small chili
1 tablespoon olive oil
4 cups (1 litre/1¾ pints) water
3 slices galangal
1 tablespoon fish sauce
3 fish steaks (any fish will do)
3 bergamot and/or coriander leaves
½ teaspoon chili paste
1 tablespoon lemon juice

Cut the lemon grass into 5-cm (2-inch) lengths. Crush the garlic, shallots and chili in a mortar, then brown them lightly in the oil before transferring them to a large pan with the water, galangal, lemon grass and fish sauce.

Bring to the boil and then add the fish steaks. Cover, and simmer for 10 minutes over medium heat.

Remove from the heat. Add the bergamot, coriander, chili paste and lemon juice.

Serve hot in large individual bowls, breaking up the fish if necessary, or in a tureen on a hot plate.

Fish Soup; Prawn Soup with Lemon Grass in the steamboat.

Tom Yam Kung

PRAWN SOUP WITH LEMON GRASS

20 prawns (shrimp)
4-5 cups (1 litre/1¾ pints) water
3 shallots, finely chopped
2 tomatoes, cut into quarters
2 stalks lemon grass, lightly pounded
2 tablespoons fish sauce
2 slices fresh or dried galangal
150 g (5 oz) straw mushrooms
6 bergamot leaves
3 tablespoons lemon juice
2-3 small chilies
pepper
Garnish:
coriander leaves or chives and parsley

Wash the prawns and shell them without removing the tails.

Pour the water into a pan, add the shallots, tomatoes, lemon grass, fish sauce and galangal. Boil for 5 minutes.

Add the prawns and mushrooms, and cook until the prawns turn pink.

Add the bergamot leaves, lemon juice and whole chilies. Season with pepper. Cover and remove from the heat.

Serve hot, sprinkling with coriander leaves or a mixture of chives and parsley.

Tom Yam Thalay

SEAFOOD SOUP WITH LEMON GRASS

Prepare the soup as for Prawn Soup with Lemon Grass (Tom Yam Kung), replacing the prawns with 500 g (1 lb) mixed fish and shellfish.

Tom Ped

DUCK SOUP

500 g (1 lb) duck meat, diced
8 cups (1.75 litres/3 pints) water
1 teaspoon pepper
8 Chinese mushrooms
2 tablespoons light soya sauce
2 tablespoons fish sauce
2 young sticks celery, roughly sliced

Wash the duck to get rid of any smell. Heat the water, and when it boils add the duck and pepper to taste. Simmer until tender, about 30 minutes.

Soak the mushrooms, discarding the stems, and add to the soup.

Add the soya sauce and fish sauce to taste. Add more water, if it has reduced a lot.

Toss the celery into the soup and remove from the heat immediately.

Tom Jued Kalampli Kung

CABBAGE AND PRAWN SOUP

4 cloves garlic, crushed
2 tablespoons oil
300 g (10 oz) prawns (shrimp), shelled
1 medium cabbage, chopped
4 cups (1 litre/1¾ pints) water
1 tablespoon fish sauce
salt
pepper
Garnish:
2 spring onions (scallions), chopped

Lightly brown half the garlic in the oil. Add the prawns and sauté them for a few minutes. Remove and drain.

Cook the cabbage in the water for 5 minutes, adding the fish sauce and the remaining garlic.

When the cabbage is cooked, add the sautéed prawns to the boiling stock.

Add salt and pepper. Cover and simmer for 3 minutes.

When serving the soup, sprinkle each bowl with the spring onion.

Hed Tom Kha

MUSHROOM AND COCONUT CREAM SOUP

2 cups (450 ml/¾ pint) coconut cream
1 teaspoon fish sauce
1 cup (250 ml/8 fl oz) water
6 slices fresh or dried galangal
2 cups (250 g/8 oz) sliced straw mushrooms
3 bergamot leaves
salt
3 tablespoons lemon juice
3 small chilies

In a saucepan over medium heat bring the coconut cream, fish sauce, water and galangal to the boil, stirring occasionally.

When the mixture is boiling, toss in the mushrooms.

Boil for a minute, stir, add the bergamot and salt to taste and remove from the heat.

Add the lemon juice and chilies just before serving hot.

Tom Yam Hed

SPICY MUSHROOM AND LEMON GRASS SOUP

2 stalks lemon grass
4 cups (1 litre/1¾ pints) chicken stock (page 34)
2 tablespoons fish sauce
700 g (1½ lb) straw mushrooms, halved
5 bergamot leaves
4 tablespoons lemon juice
4 small chilies
Garnish:
2 spring onions (scallions), chopped

Cut the lemon grass into 2.5-cm (1-inch) lengths. Heat the stock with the lemon grass and fish sauce. Boil for 2 minutes.

Add the mushrooms. Cover and simmer for 5 minutes.

Stir in the bergamot, lemon juice and whole chilies.

Remove from heat and serve sprinkled with the spring onion.

Kaeng Liang

VEGETABLE SOUP WITH PRAWNS

1 tablespoon dried shrimp
10 shallots
10 peppercorns
2 tablespoons fish sauce
4 cups (1 litre/1¾ pints) chicken stock (page 34)
2 courgettes (zucchini)
12 small carrots
1 handful French beans
¼ cauliflower
12 prawns (shrimp)
Garnish:
basil leaves

Grind together the dried shrimp, shallots and peppercorns.

Add the fish sauce and the ground mixture to the stock. Bring to the boil and simmer while you prepare the vegetables. Dice or slice the courgettes and carrots, slice the beans, divide the cauliflower into florets.

Add the vegetables to the stock and cook for 4-5 minutes.

Shell the prawns, leaving the tails on, and add to the soup.

Simmer for a few minutes, until the prawns turn pink and the vegetables are tender. Cover and remove from the heat.

Sprinkle with a few leaves of basil and serve hot.

Vegetable Soup with Prawns

Pumpkin Soup with Coconut Cream

Kaeng Liang Fak Thong

PUMPKIN SOUP WITH COCONUT CREAM

350 g (12 oz) pumpkin, peeled
1 tablespoon lemon juice
125g (4 oz) prawns (shrimp), shelled
2 shallots, chopped
1 tablespoon shrimp paste
2 small chilies
1 large glass water
3 cups (750 ml/1¼ pints) coconut cream
pepper
1 cup basil leaves

Remove the seeds from the pumpkin and dice the flesh. Sprinkle with the lemon juice.

Pound the prawns with the shallots, shrimp paste and chilies, adding a little of the water if necessary, to form a well-mixed paste.

Pour half the coconut cream into a pan. Add the prawn mixture and bring to the boil.

Reduce the heat and stir with a wooden spoon to ensure a smooth consistency.

Add the pumpkin and cook gently for 10 minutes. Pour in the remaining coconut cream and water. Season with pepper. Cover.

Simmer for about a further 10 minutes until the pumpkin is tender but not mushy. Stir in the basil leaves and serve immediately.

Kuoy Tiao Nua

BEEF NOODLE SOUP

5 cups (1.2 litres/2 pints) beef stock (page 34)
2 cloves garlic
2 sticks celery
2 tablespoons fish sauce
2 tablespoons light soya sauce
pepper, to taste
300 g (10 oz) beef fillet, cut into thin strips
500 g (1 lb) rice noodles
1 tablespoon chopped garlic
2 tablespoons oil
½ tablespoon chopped coriander leaves
½ tablespoon chopped spring onion (scallion)
chili powder, to taste
2 tablespoons lemon juice or vinegar

Heat the stock with the whole garlic cloves, celery, fish sauce, soya sauce and pepper. Cover and simmer for 10 minutes.

Remove the garlic and celery. Bring the stock to a full boil.

Place the beef in a straining spoon or strainer and hold in the boiling stock for 30 seconds. Remove and drain. Reduce the heat.

Cook the noodles in the simmering stock for 2 minutes, then remove and drain them. Meanwhile lightly brown the chopped garlic in the oil.

Serve the soup in individual bowls. First place the noodles in each bowl and sprinkle with the coriander, spring onion, browned garlic, chili powder and pepper. Add the meat, a few drops of lemon juice or vinegar and the stock.

Kai Tom Khing

CHICKEN SOUP WITH LEMON AND GINGER

2 tablespoons olive oil
1 clove garlic, chopped
350 g (12 oz) chicken breast, diced
4 cups (1 litre/1¾ pints) water
25 g (4 oz) straw mushrooms, chopped
2 tablespoons lemon juice
2 small green chilies, sliced in rings
2 spring onions (scallions), chopped
1 pinch ground ginger
Garnish:
coriander leaves

Heat the oil in a saucepan or wok and fry the garlic until soft but not brown.

Add the chicken and stir-fry for 5 minutes. Cool a little.

Add the water and mushrooms. Bring to the boil and simmer for 10 minutes. Add the lemon juice. Cover, and cook gently for a further 10 minutes.

Add the chilies, spring onions and ginger. Remove from the heat. Sprinkle with coriander leaves before serving.

Kaeng Jued Nor Mai Kai

CHICKEN SOUP WITH BAMBOO SHOOTS

400 g (14 oz) bamboo shoots, chopped
4 cups (1 litre/1¾ pints) chicken stock (page 34)
200 g (7 oz) chicken breast, diced
2 tablespoons fish sauce
5 peppercorns, freshly ground

Fresh bamboo shoots must be boiled for 30 minutes before use. Canned bamboo shoots do not need precooking.

Heat the stock. When it begins to simmer, add the chicken, bamboo shoots, fish sauce and pepper. Cook for a few minutes — just long enough to cook the chicken.

Kaeng Jued Tao Hoo

BEANCURD SOUP
WITH PORK

250 g (8 oz) beancurd
200 g (7 oz) beansprouts
200 g (7 oz) pork, minced or ground
salt
pepper
4 cups (1 litre/1¾ pints) pork stock (page 34)
2 cloves garlic, crushed
1 tablespoon fish sauce
2 spring onions (scallions), sliced into rounds

Cut the beancurd into squares. Wash the beansprouts and remove the roots. Make the pork into small balls, seasoning with salt and pepper.

Bring the stock or water to the boil with the garlic and the fish sauce.

Add the pork balls, beancurd and the beansprouts. Simmer for 3-5 minutes over medium heat, then add the spring onions.

Stir, add salt and pepper to taste and remove from the heat.

Kaeng Jued Wun Sen

MINCED PORK AND
NOODLE SOUP

50 g (2 oz) Chinese mushrooms
50 g (2 oz) bean thread or rice vermicelli
1 tablespoon chopped coriander root
5 cloves garlic
½ teaspoon black pepper
2 tablespoons oil
200 g (7 oz) pork, minced or ground
3 cups (750 ml/1¼ pints) pork stock (page 34)
2 tablespoons fish sauce
2 spring onions (scallions), coarsely chopped
Garnish:
coriander leaves

Soak the mushrooms in lukewarm water for 30 minutes, and the vermicelli for 10 minutes. Cut the vermicelli into 8-cm (3-inch) lengths.

Pound or mince (grind) the coriander root with the garlic and pepper.

Lightly brown the mixture in the oil over medium heat.

Add the pork and stir-fry for 2 minutes. Pour in ½ cup (125 ml/4 fl oz) stock and the fish sauce and mushrooms. Cook for 5 minutes over low heat.

Add the rest of the stock and the noodles. Cook for 5 minutes.

Remove from the heat. Add the spring onions and cover.

Before serving, sprinkle each bowl of soup with coriander leaves.

Kaeng Jued Sakhou

TAPIOCA SOUP

5 cups (1.25 litres/2 pints) pork stock (page 34)
½ cup (125 g/4 oz) minced or ground pork
1 tablespoon chopped garlic
3 tablespoons fish sauce
½ cup (75 g/3 oz) tapioca
½ cup (125 g/4 oz) cooked/canned crab meat
pepper
Garnish:
4 lettuce leaves, roughly chopped
12 coriander leaves

Heat the stock to simmering point in a large pan. Pour ½ cup of the hot stock into a bowl and stir in the pork. Return the mixture to the pan.

Add the garlic and fish sauce to taste, then add the tapioca and cook for 5-10 minutes. When the tapioca is clear, add the crab meat, and season to taste with pepper. Remove from the heat. Line individual soup bowls with the lettuce. Pour in the soup and sprinkle with coriander leaves.

Fish and Seafood

Fish and Seafood

The love the Thais have for fish and seafood is born from nature's bounty. Their coastline along the Andaman Sea and the Gulf of Thailand is long, the country is traversed from north to south by wide rivers full of fish, and the plains are criss-crossed with a maze of canals. Amateur and professional fishermen can be seen everywhere, as they cast, haul in and lift their nets.

The Thais eat far more fish than meat, and in the Thai diet the produce of the sea and rivers is second only to rice in importance. An old Thai saying, "There is rice in the fields, and fish in the water", sums up how the Thais measure happiness and illustrates how they appreciate their natural good fortune. Inland, freshwater fish is available throughout the country. Sea fish is often preserved by smoking, salting or drying, and in the markets, highly aromatic dried fish and cuttlefish are displayed in bamboo boxes or hanging from wires.

Fresh fish can be fried, steamed or wrapped in a banana leaf and cooked over a charcoal fire. It is not salted before being cooked in these ways; instead each piece is dipped in a sauce served as an accompaniment to the meal. The sauces are made from different combinations of hot, salty, sour and sweet ingredients such as chilies, fish sauce, shrimp paste, tamarind or lemon juice, and sugar (see Sauces chapter). The Thais also eat a great quantity of seafood — prawns, shrimp, crabs, squid, mussels, cockles etc. — in salads or grilled. Practically every day Thais partake of seafood feasts as normal meals. Thailand has made the most of this abundance by developing one of the best shrimp and prawn industries in the region, and relies on this as one of its principal exports.

Both fish and seafood are made into delicious curries and wonderful soups. In addition, they are the main ingredients of those two basic Thai condiments, "nam pla" (fish sauce) and "kapi" (shrimp paste).

The seafood recipes in this book should not present any problems in the West as fresh or frozen varieties are available internationally nowadays. The fish recipes will be extra tasty if prepared with cold-water species as these usually have more flavour than their warm-water cousins.

Pla Thord Rad Sauce Priew Wan

SWEET AND SOUR LEMON SOLE

700 g (1½ lb) lemon sole
1 cup (250 ml/8 fl oz) milk
7 tablespoons oil
2 cloves garlic, crushed
1 small red chili, crushed
3 shallots, crushed
1 tablespoon fish sauce
2 tablespoons sugar
1 tablespoon tamarind juice or vinegar

Wash and gut the fish, then soak it in the milk for 1 hour. Drain.

Fry the fish in 6 tablespoons hot oil until it turns golden. Remove it from the pan and keep warm.

Sauté the garlic, chili and shallots in 1 tablespoon oil until lightly browned. Add the fish sauce, sugar and tamarind juice.

Pour this sauce on the cooked fish and serve hot.

Pla Thord Rad Khing

FRIED FISH WITH GINGER

1 × 1 kg (2 lb) meaty white fish
8 tablespoons oil
3 cloves garlic, chopped
2 tablespoons grated ginger
2 slices ham, cut into strips
2 tablespoons fish sauce
1 teaspoon sugar
2 teaspoons pepper
8 tablespoons water
Garnish:
2 spring onions (scallions), in short lengths

Wash and gut the fish. Score on both sides and fry in the oil until golden brown on both sides. Put aside and keep hot.

In the same oil, brown the garlic and ginger. Add the ham and sauté for 2 minutes. Add the fish sauce, sugar, pepper and water. Mix well and bring to the boil.

Pour this sauce over the fish and sprinkle with spring onions.

Kaeng Som

SWEET AND SOUR FISH CURRY

2 × 200 g (7 oz) white fish fillets
3 cups (750 ml/1¼ pints) water
5 red chilies, fresh or dried
5 shallots
1 teaspoon shrimp paste
1 teaspoon salt
125 g (4 oz) green beans, in short lengths
125 g (4 oz) white cabbage, chopped
200 g (7 oz) courgettes (zucchini), cubed
3 tablespoons tamarind juice
3 tablespoons fish sauce
1 tablespoon sugar

Cut one of the fish fillets into cubes and keep the other one whole.

Boil the whole fish fillet in the water over strong heat for 5 minutes. Reduce the heat and simmer while preparing the other ingredients.

Pound together the chilies, shallots and shrimp paste. Add the salt.

Drain the fish, reserving the stock, and add the cooked fish fillet to the chili mixture. Pound together until a smooth paste is obtained.

Add this paste to the reserved fish stock and bring to the boil.

Add the cubed fish and vegetables, then the tamarind juice, fish sauce and sugar. Bring to the boil. Lower the heat, cover and simmer for 5 minutes.

This curry can be served as a soup or with Plain Rice (Khao Suoy).

71

Grouper with Ginger

Steamed Mussels

Pla Phad Khing

GROUPER WITH GINGER

8 Chinese mushrooms (optional)
600 g (1¼ lb) grouper, bass or
other meaty white fish fillets
4 cloves garlic, chopped
3 tablespoons shredded ginger
oil for frying
125 g (4 oz) canned soya beans
3 chilies, cut into strips
4 spring onions (scallions), in short lengths
1 tablespoon fish sauce
1 teaspoon sugar
Garnish:
coriander leaves

Soak the mushrooms in warm water for 30 minutes, if using.

Cut the fish fillets into bite-sized pieces. Brown the garlic and ginger in a little oil for 3-4 minutes.

Add the fish, mushrooms and soya beans. Cover and cook for 5 minutes.

Mix together the chilies, spring onions, fish sauce and sugar and add this to the fish. Mix well and cook for a further 2 minutes.

Serve sprinkled with coriander leaves.

Hoy Mang Phou Nueng

STEAMED MUSSELS

2 kg (4½ lb) mussels
1 cup basil leaves
4 spring onions (scallions), in short lengths
Sauce:
½ cup (125 ml/4 fl oz) lemon juice
2 tablespoons fish sauce
1 teaspoon sugar
2 coriander roots, coarsely chopped
2 cloves garlic, crushed
1 teaspoon ground paprika
½ cup (125 ml/4 fl oz) water

Wash and scrape the mussels. Discard any open ones. Place in a steamer over boiling water and sprinkle with the basil leaves and spring onions.

Steam for 10 minutes. Remove from the heat and wait for 2 more minutes before opening the steamer.

Meanwhile, mix the sauce ingredients together, bring to the boil then leave to cool.

Serve the mussels in a large dish, discarding any that have not opened during steaming. An individual dish of the sauce should be given to each diner.

Kung Thord Krathiam Prik Thai

SAUTÉED PRAWNS WITH GARLIC AND PEPPER

800 g (1¾ lb) prawns (shrimp)
6 coriander roots, finely chopped
5 cloves garlic, crushed
1 tablespoon salt
1 tablespoon pepper
½ cup (125 ml/4 fl oz) oil
1 tablespoon fish sauce
Garnish:
¼ red pepper, cut into thin strips
coriander leaves

Shell the prawns, leaving the tails on. Put the prawns in a bowl with the coriander root, garlic, salt and pepper. Mix thoroughly and leave to rest for 1 hour.

Drain the prawns. Fry them in the oil over medium heat for 2 minutes on each side. Drain and keep warm.

Pour the marinade remaining in the bowl into the oil used for frying the prawns and simmer on low heat. Add the fish sauce and mix well.

Pour the sauce over the prawns. Sprinkle with red pepper and coriander leaves.

Pla Nueg Phad Prik

SAUTÉED CUTTLEFISH WITH FRESH CHILIES

800 g (1¾ lb) cuttlefish
2 tablespoons chopped garlic
2 shallots, chopped
2 tablespoons oil
2 fresh chilies, chopped
2 spring onions (scallions), sliced into rings
2 teaspoons fish sauce
2 teaspoons oyster sauce
salt
pepper
1 teaspoon chopped coriander leaves

Wash the cuttlefish and cut it into small pieces. Bring a pan of water to simmering point and poach the cuttlefish for 3 minutes. Drain and put aside.

Brown the garlic and shallots in the oil. Add, in order, the chilies, spring onions, cuttlefish, fish sauce and oyster sauce. Add salt and pepper to taste.

Saute the mixture for 5 minutes. Mix in the coriander.

Serve with Plain Rice (Khao Suoy).

Kung Phad Takrai Sai Thua

SAUTÉED PRAWNS WITH MUSHROOMS

1 tablespoon finely chopped lemon grass
1 tablespoon finely chopped garlic
2 teaspoons pepper
1 teaspoon salt
8 tablespoons oil
700 g (1½ lb) prawns (shrimp), shelled
125 g (4 oz) cup mushrooms
125 g (4 oz) string beans, cut into three
3 tablespoons fish sauce
1 tablespoon sugar
1 tablespoon flour

Garnish:
½ cup crushed peanuts
3 fresh chilies, chopped
¼ green pepper (capsicum), cut into strips
chopped spring onions (scallions)

Pound together the lemon grass, garlic, pepper and salt to produce a paste.

Brown this paste in the oil over medium heat for a few minutes.

Turn up the heat and add the prawns, mushrooms and beans. Sauté for 3 minutes.

Add the fish sauce, sugar and the flour blended with a little water. Mix well.

Serve sprinkled with the peanuts, chilies, green pepper and spring onions.

Hoy Marng Phou Ob

MUSSELS WITH LEMON GRASS

2 kg (4½ lb) mussels
2 cups (450 ml/¾ pint) water
4 shallots, finely sliced
2 stalks lemon grass
2 tablespoons fish sauce
salt
pepper
1 cup basil leaves

Wash and scrape the mussels. Discard any open ones.

Bring the water to the boil in a large saucepan, then add the shallots, lemon grass and fish sauce.

When the water comes to the boil again, add the mussels. Cover and boil for 5 minutes over strong heat.

Add salt and pepper to taste, and sprinkle with basil leaves. Cover, and cook for a few minutes before removing from the heat.

Before serving, discard any mussels which have not opened during cooking.

Steamed Fish (left) with Spicy Tomato Sauce (below right);
Sautéed Prawns with Lemon Grass (centre); Stuffed Crab accompanied by Chili Sauce.

Chou Chi Kung

SAUTÉED PRAWNS WITH LEMON GRASS

2 cups (450 ml/¾ pint) coconut milk
1 fresh chili, chopped
1 teaspoon finely chopped galangal
1 tablespoon finely chopped lemon grass
2 teaspoons chopped coriander root
4 cloves garlic, chopped
3 shallots, chopped
1 teaspoon shrimp paste
2 tablespoons fish sauce
1 tablespoon brown sugar
800 g (1¾ lb) prawns (shrimp), shelled
Garnish:
1 tablespoon shredded bergamot leaves
¼ red pepper (capsicum), cut in thin strips

Pour the coconut milk into a pan and simmer over a low heat for 8 minutes.

Pound together the chili, galangal, lemon grass, coriander, garlic, shallots and shrimp paste with just enough water to form a paste.

Add this paste to the coconut milk, mix thoroughly and increase the heat.

Add the fish sauce and the sugar and simmer on medium heat for a few minutes, stirring all the time.

When the sauce starts to thicken, add the prawns, mix thoroughly and simmer until the prawns turn pink and are cooked. The time for this will vary according to the size of the prawns.

Sprinkle with bergamot and red pepper. Serve with Plain Rice (Khao Suoy).

Pla Nueng Jaew Makhua Tet

STEAMED FISH WITH SPICY TOMATO SAUCE

1 × 1½ kg (3 lb) whole fish
3 coriander roots
4 cloves garlic
5 peppercorns
3 tomatoes
2 chilies
6 shallots, unpeeled
1 whole head garlic
1 tablespoon lemon juice
2 tablespoons fish sauce

Clean, gut and score the fish. Pound together the coriander root, garlic cloves and peppercorns. Rub the resulting paste into the fish.

Lightly burn the tomatoes, chilies, shallots and garlic head, either in the oven or on foil over direct heat. Remove the burnt skins and chop the flesh coarsely. Mix it with the lemon juice and fish sauce and put to one side.

Steam the fish for 20 minutes. Arrange on a bed of steamed vegetables of your choice and serve with the reserved spicy tomato sauce.

Pou Cha

STUFFED CRAB

1 tablespoon chopped garlic
1 tablespoon chopped coriander root
10 peppercorns
2 onions, chopped
1 tablespoon fish sauce
200 g (7 oz) pork, minced or ground
500 g (1 lb) cooked or canned crab meat
4-6 crab shells
4-6 sprigs coriander leaves
2 egg yolks
oil for deep-frying

Pound together the garlic, coriander root, peppercorns and onion with the fish sauce. Mix in the pork then knead in the mashed crab meat.

Fill the crab shells with this mixture. Place in a steamer over boiling water and steam for 15 minutes, then top with coriander leaves and coat with egg yolk.

Heat enough oil to deep-fry the stuffed shells. When the oil is hot, drop in the stuffed shells, and cook until the tops turn brown.

Garnish with salad ingredients and serve with Chili Sauce (Nam Prik Khee Ka).

Yam Thalay

SEAFOOD SALAD

12 large prawns (shrimp)
4 cuttlefish, cut into small pieces
1 kg (2 lb) mussels
4 small chilies
2 onions, finely sliced
4 cloves garlic, crushed
1 tablespoon salt
3 tablespoons lemon juice
To serve:
6 lettuce leaves
10 coriander leaves
1 tablespoon bergamot leaves, cut into strips
2 red chilies, cut into flowers (see page 22)

Shell the prawns but leave the tails on. Poach the prawns and cuttlefish for 3 minutes. Drain.

Scrub the mussels and discard any open ones. Place in a saucepan containing 1 cm (½ inch) water, cover and cook the mussels over moderate heat for about 5 minutes until the shells open. Discard any which have not opened. Take the mussels out of their shells and mix them with the cuttlefish and prawns in a bowl.

Tenderize the chilies by pressing them with the back of a spoon. Add the onion, chilies, garlic, salt and lemon juice to the seafood.

Serve on a bed of lettuce leaves, sprinkled with coriander and bergamot leaves and chili flowers.

Kung Phad Nam Prik Phao

SAUTÉED PRAWNS WITH MILD CHILI PASTE

12 large prawns (shrimp)
4 cloves garlic, crushed
salt
7 tablespoons oil
2 tablespoons burnt mild chili paste
1 tablespoon fish sauce
4 bergamot leaves, finely chopped
½ red chili, chopped

Shell the prawns, leaving the tails on. Roll the prawns in the garlic and salt and leave for 10 minutes. Heat the oil in a pan and sauté the prawns for 3-4 minutes. Remove the prawns with a slotted spoon and place them in a serving dish. Keep them warm.

Over low heat dilute the chili paste in about 1 tablespoon of the oil left in the pan and simmer for 2 minutes. Then stir in the fish sauce.

Pour the sauce over the prawns and sprinkle with the bergamot and red chili.

Kung Nam Daeng

PRAWNS WITH WHITE CABBAGE

6 Chinese mushrooms
1 white cabbage
3 tablespoons oil
4 slices smoked ham, quartered
12 large prawns (shrimp), shelled
200 g (7 oz) cooked or canned crab meat
Sauce:
1 tablespoon flour
2 tablespoons oil
2 teaspoons sesame seed oil
1 teaspoon rice wine
1 teaspoon oyster sauce
1 teaspoon light soya sauce
1 cup (250 ml/8 fl oz) pork stock (page 34)

Soak the mushrooms in warm water for 30 minutes. Blanch about 15 cabbage leaves in a pan of boiling water for 1 minute and drain and pat dry. Brown them lightly in 1 tablespoon hot oil. Add a few drops of water and cover. Cook over low heat for 5-6 minutes, remove and arrange on a serving dish.

Brown the ham in another tablespoon oil. Arrange on the cabbage leaves.

Add the remaining oil to the same pan and fry the prawns. Place on top of the ham.

Mix the ingredients for the sauce and bring to the boil. Add the crab meat and drained mushrooms and mix well. Cook for 3-4 minutes and pour over the prawns.

Kung Thord

COCONUT FRIED PRAWNS

750 g (1½ lb) prawns (shrimp)
2 shallots, chopped
2 cloves garlic, chopped
2 teaspoons crushed galangal
2 tablespoons chopped lemon grass
1 teaspoon chopped coriander root
1 tablespoon lemon juice
2 cups (450 ml/¾ pint) coconut cream
1 teaspoon salt
2 cups (250 g/8 oz) flour
oil for frying

Shell the prawns, leaving the tails on. Pound together the shallots, garlic, galangal, lemon grass and coriander root. Add the lemon juice, coconut cream and salt.

Marinate the prawns in this mixture for 30 minutes, then drain the prawns and roll them in the flour.

Over strong heat fry the prawns in the oil until they turn pink.

Plain Rice (Khao Suoy) and Aubergine Fritters (Makhua Chub Khai Thord) go well with this dish.

Kung Phao Nam Pla Wan   Sweet and Sour Prawns

SWEET AND SOUR PRAWNS

4 tablespoons tamarind or lemon juice
4 tablespoons sugar
2 tablespoons fish sauce
2 cloves garlic, finely chopped
2 shallots, sliced
2 tablespoons oil
4 small dried chilies (optional)
1 kg (2 lb) large prawns (shrimp)

Mix together in a pan the tamarind juice, sugar and fish sauce. Bring to the boil and simmer until the liquid thickens. Transfer to a dish and keep warm.

Brown the garlic and shallots in the oil. Drain and add to the sauce, reserving the cooking oil.

In the reserved oil, fry the whole chilies, if using. Add them to the sauce.

Cook the prawns under the grill (broiler) or over a barbecue until they turn pink. The time taken will vary according to the size of the prawns.

Serve the prawns with the sauce, or shell the prawns and serve them in the sauce.

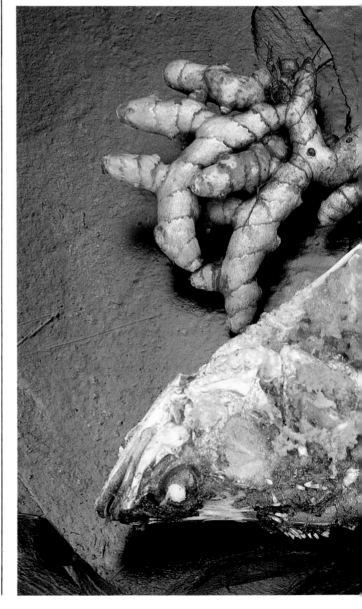

80

Cockles with Basil

Fried Prawns on Omelette Web

Southern Thai Fried Fish

Hoy Lai Phad Nam Prik Phao

COCKLES WITH BASIL

4 cloves garlic, crushed
2 shallots, crushed
½ cup (125 ml/4 fl oz) oil
3 red chilies
3 green or yellow chilies
1 teaspoon burnt mild chili paste
1 kg (2 lb) cockles, scrubbed
15 basil leaves
1 tablespoon fish sauce

In a large frying pan, brown the garlic and shallots in the oil.

Tenderize the chilies by pressing them with the back of a spoon then add them, whole, to the garlic and shallots. Stir in the burnt mild chili paste.

Add the cockles and cook for 3 minutes over strong heat, stirring all the time. Add most of the basil leaves and the fish sauce and mix well. Remove from the heat. Garnish with the remaining basil leaves.

Serve hot with Plain Rice (Khao Suoy).

Kung Thord Khai

FRIED PRAWNS ON OMELETTE WEB

6 jumbo-size prawns (shrimp)
2 eggs
oil for frying
2 cloves garlic, crushed
1 coriander root, crushed
10 peppercorns, crushed

Shell and clean the prawns, leaving on the heads and tails. Cut them lengthways down the middle. Use the eggs to make 3 omelette webs (page 34).

Fry the prawns in the hot oil and then drain them and place them in pairs on the omelette webs.

Brown the garlic, coriander root and pepper in the oil remaining in the pan. Drain and sprinkle over the prawns.

Pla Thord Pak Thai

SOUTHERN THAI FRIED FISH

1 × 1½ kg (3 lb) carp or 8 fish fillets
10 thin slices turmeric or root ginger
6 cloves garlic
3 stalks lemon grass, chopped
1 teaspoon salt
1 teaspoon pepper
8 tablespoons oil

Wash the fish and gut if necessary. Pound together the turmeric, garlic, lemon grass, salt and pepper. Coat the fish with half of this mixture, and leave for 1 hour.

Fry the fish in the oil until golden brown. Remove from the oil.

Brown the remaining turmeric mixture in the oil left in the pan to make a sauce to serve with the fish.

Kaeng Chak Som

FISH CURRY

6 large dried chilies
1 teaspoon shrimp paste
5 shallots, chopped
1 teaspoon coarse salt
3 cups (750 ml/1¼ pints) water
1 tablespoon tamarind juice
3 tablespoons fish sauce
6 fillets sea fish (about 1 kg/2 lb)
6 bergamot leaves
1 bergamot or 1 lemon, peeled and halved

Cut the chilies into pieces, and soak them in water for 10 minutes to soften. Grind or pound the chilies with the shrimp paste, shallots and salt. Mix this paste with the water and bring to the boil.

When boiling, stir in the tamarind juice and fish sauce. Add the fish fillets, bergamot leaves and fruit. Cook for 15-20 minutes, and then remove from the heat. Serve with Plain Rice (Khao Suoy).

Pou Phad Kari

CRAB CURRY

4 crabs
3 cloves garlic, crushed
3 tablespoons oil
4 small red chilies
1 teaspoon crushed ginger
1 tablespoon canned soya beans
1 teaspoon curry powder
1 tablespoon oyster sauce
1 tablespoon flour, blended with
2 tablespoons water
½ teaspoon salt
6 spring onions (scallions) in short lengths
3 sticks celery, in short lengths

Put the crabs in the freezer for 15 minutes to firm up the flesh. Wash them thoroughly.

Cut the crabs in half through the centre of the shell from head to rear. Remove part of the soft undershell and scrape out the inedible parts. Cut the ends off the legs and break the pincers. Wash again and drain.

Brown the garlic in the oil. Tenderize the chilies by pressing them with the back of a spoon then add the chilies, ginger, soya beans and curry to the garlic and mix well.

Add the crabs and sauté over strong heat until they turn red.

Add the oyster sauce, blended flour and salt and cook for 2 minutes, stirring occasionally.

Add the spring onions and celery, stir well and cook for a moment more.

Pla Rad Prik

FRIED FISH WITH CHILI SAUCE

1 × 500 g (1 lb) meaty white fish
1 teaspoon salt
1 teaspoon pepper
2 tablespoons flour
oil for deep-frying
4 cloves garlic, finely chopped
1 chili, chopped
1 teaspoon vinegar
1 teaspoon sugar
1-2 tablespoons water
Garnish:
½ red pepper (capsicum), finely chopped
1 cucumber, sliced into rounds
2 tomatoes, thinly sliced

Wash and gut the fish. Score on both sides. Sprinkle the fish with salt and pepper then roll it in the flour.

Deep-fry the fish in the oil over strong heat until golden brown.

Make the sauce by first browning the garlic and chili in a little fresh oil over low heat. Add salt, vinegar, sugar and water. Simmer until the sauce caramelizes.

Pour the sauce over the fish and sprinkle with red pepper. Arrange slices of cucumber and tomato around the fish.

Vegetables and Salads

Vegetables and Salads

Vegetables play an important part in Thai nutrition. Although Thais do not fully practise the vegetarianism preached by Buddhism, and they do eat meat (as long as the animals are sacrificed by non-Buddhists), they do so in small quantities.

Nature produces vegetables in plenty and in a temptingly wide variety of colours and shapes — tomatoes, cucumbers, shallots, crispy lettuce, pure white cauliflowers, green beans, peppers, courgettes (zucchini), pumpkins and so on. New species are regularly introduced. They grow on the fertile watered lands around Bangkok as well as on the hill slopes of the north. As well as these familiar ones, Thais also consume many vegetables which are unknown in the West, and translations might not always be available for some of them. They include aquatic plants such as "phak bung", creeping plants like "tam lung", rhizomes like the white turmeric, bamboo shoots and lotus stems.

Fruit is often used in salads — a particular favourite is papaya — and a great number of salad and vegetable dishes include fish, seafood or meat. Salads are refreshing in the hot, humid climate of Thailand and in one form or another — from a simple dish of raw beans to a complicated restaurant showpiece — appear at most meal times. They are not served at any particular moment during the meal. They come with all the other dishes and people nibble at them while eating curries or other hot courses. Sometimes they can be meals in themselves.

Oil and vinegar are rarely used to prepare dressings for salads. The most common dressing recipes include lemon juice, chilies, fish sauce and shallots. Papaya salad is served with a dressing of pounded peanuts, fish sauce, garlic and chopped chilies with dried prawns (shrimp). Another popular salad dressing is made with hard-boiled egg yolks mashed in tepid water together with sugar and lemon juice. As with their other sauces, the Thais create a wide range of salad dressings from different combinations of all the available ingredients.

Vegetables, raw or lightly cooked, are also eaten with "nam prik" (see Sauces chapter). Sometimes they are steamed the Chinese way, or sometimes fried, but however they are prepared they should never be overcooked. They must remain crunchy and full of flavour.

Raw vegetables and fruit are often skilfully carved into baskets, flowers and other exquisite shapes for special occasions. An introduction to this art is given on page 19.

Phad Phak Ruam Mit

SAUTÉED VEGETABLES

75 g (3 oz) bamboo shoots
300 g (10 oz) whole baby corn
125 g (4 oz) asparagus tips
250 g (8 oz) snow peas (mange-tout)
150 g (5 oz) young carrots
125 g (4 oz) straw mushrooms
4 spring onions (scallions)
½ cup (125 ml/4 fl oz) vegetable oil
3 cloves garlic, chopped
75 g (3 oz) bamboo shoots
2 tablespoons fish sauce
1 teaspoon sesame seed oil
pepper
salt

Boil the bamboo shoots for 30 minutes if fresh or 10 minutes if canned. Cut them into slivers. Rinse and drain the baby corn, asparagus and snow peas. Slice the carrots into rounds. Cut the mushrooms in half and the spring onions into short lengths.

Heat the vegetable oil over strong heat and fry the garlic until browned. Remove the garlic from the oil and leave to one side.

Stir-fry the corn, carrots and bamboo shoots in the same oil for 2 to 3 minutes, gradually adding in the fish sauce and sesame seed oil.

Throw in the remaining vegetables, together with the browned garlic, pepper and salt. Fry for a further 2 minutes. Serve hot.

Makhua Chub Khai Thord

AUBERGINE FRITTERS

2 eggs, beaten
salt to taste
2 tablespoons milk
2 aubergines (eggplants), finely sliced
oil for deep-frying

Mix the eggs, salt and milk together to make a batter. Dip the aubergine slices into the batter and deep-fry the coated aubergine slices in the oil over moderate heat until evenly brown.

Prik Wan Sord Sai

STUFFED PEPPERS

6 medium peppers (capsicums)
300 g (10 oz) prawns (shrimp), shelled
500 g (1 lb) pork, minced or ground
3 tablespoons chopped spring onions (scallions)
2 tablespoons chopped garlic
1 teaspoon chopped ginger
1 tablespoon light soya sauce
pepper to taste
1 tablespoon cornflour, dissolved in
3 tablespoons cold water

Cut the tops off the peppers and put aside to be used as lids. Scoop out the insides of the peppers. Chop the prawns.

Mix the pork, prawns, spring onions, garlic, ginger, soya sauce and pepper with the blended cornflour. Use this mixture to stuff the peppers, then replace the tops. Cook in a moderate oven (180°C/350°F/Gas Mark 4) for 30 minutes.

Serve hot, accompanied by Fish Sauce with Small Chilies (Nam Pla Prik Kheenon).

Phad Phak Nam Man Hoy

SAUTÉED VEGETABLES IN OYSTER SAUCE

2 tablespoons chopped garlic
4 tablespoons oil
600 g (1¼ lb) sliced vegetables —
cabbage, broccoli, courgettes (zucchini),
Brussels sprouts
1 tablespoon light soya sauce
5 tablespoons oyster sauce
pepper

Brown the garlic in the oil over strong heat. Add the vegetables and stir vigorously. Moisten with a little water if they seem dry. Cover for a few seconds. Stir in the soya sauce and oyster sauce with pepper to taste. Cover and cook for 3 minutes over medium heat.

Serve as an accompaniment to a meat dish.

Stuffed Mild Chilies

Prik Yuak Sod Sai

STUFFED MILD CHILIES

500 g (1 lb) pork, minced or ground
5 eggs
1 tablespoon crushed garlic
2 tablespoons chopped onion
1 tablespoon chopped coriander leaves
1 teaspoon pepper
salt
8-12 mild chilies
Garnish:
1 chili flower (page 22)

Mix together the pork, 1 egg, the garlic, onion and coriander. Add the pepper and salt to taste.

Cut the tops off the chilies, scoop out the seeds and stuff the chilies with the pork mixture. Steam them for 10-12 minutes.

Make omelette webs (page 34) with the remaining 4 eggs and roll the stuffed chilies in them. Arrange the stuffed chilies on a plate and garnish with a chili flower.

Crab and Pork Stuffed Tomatoes

Fish Stuffed Peppers

Aubergine with Pork and Prawns, before garnishing.

Makhua Phao Song Kruang

AUBERGINE WITH PORK AND PRAWNS

3-4 large aubergines (eggplants)
150 g (5 oz) pork, minced or ground
200 g (7 oz) prawns (shrimp), shelled
½ teaspoon pepper
3 shallots, chopped
1 tablespoon oil
4 cloves garlic, crushed
1 tablespoon vinegar
1 tablespoon fish sauce
2 tablespoons fermented soya beans
1 teaspoon sugar
Garnish:
1 red pepper (capsicum) or 3 red chilies

Cook the aubergines whole in a hot oven (230°C/450°F/Gas Mark 8) or barbecue them directly over strong heat until the skins are burnt.

Toss the aubergines into cold water then peel and cut them into large pieces. Place the pieces in a serving dish.

Mix the pork and prawns together. Add pepper to taste and put aside.

Sauté the shallots in the oil. Remove the shallots and drain them, using the oil remaining in the pan to sauté the garlic. When the garlic is golden brown, add the pork and prawn mixture and sauté for a few minutes over medium heat.

Add the vinegar, fish sauce, soya beans and sugar and mix in well; cover and cook for a few minutes.

Top the aubergine pieces with the pork and prawn mixture, and sprinkle with the shallots and strips of pepper or chili.

Makhua Tet Sawoiel

CRAB AND PORK STUFFED TOMATOES

10 tomatoes
salt
3 coriander roots, chopped
4 cloves garlic, chopped
10 peppercorns
250 g (8 oz) pork, minced or ground
250 g (8 oz) cooked or canned crab meat
2 tablespoons chopped onion
1 teaspoon sugar
2 tablespoons fish sauce
5 eggs

Cut the tops off the tomatoes and put them aside to be used as lids. Scoop out the flesh of the tomatoes. Coat the insides of the tomato shells lightly with salt and stand upside down to allow excess water to run out.

Pound together the coriander roots, garlic and peppercorns. Add the pork, crab, onion, sugar, fish sauce and 1 egg. Mix well together.

Stuff the rinsed and dried tomatoes with the mixture and replace the lids on top.

Cook in a medium oven (180°C/350°F/Gas Mark 4) for 30 minutes.

Roll the cooked, stuffed tomatoes in omelette webs (page 34) made from the 4 remaining eggs before serving with a sauce of your choice.

Hor Mok Pla

FISH STUFFED PEPPERS

6-9 large green peppers (capsicums)
800 g (1¾ lb) filleted white fish
2 tablespoons fish sauce
½ cup (125 ml/4 fl oz) sour cream
2 tablespoons red curry paste (page 42)
1 egg, separated
Garnish:
1 spring onion (scallion), shredded
1 red chili, shredded

90

Slice the tops off the peppers and put them aside to be used as lids, or cut the peppers in half lengthways. Scoop the insides out of the peppers.

Chop the fish roughly and mash it with the fish sauce, sour cream and curry paste. Finally, stir in the egg yolk.

Stuff the peppers with the fish mixture. Place a teaspoon of beaten egg white on each and sprinkle with shreds of spring onion and chili. Replace the tops as lids, if using, and steam for 30 minutes.

Phad Makhua Sai Thua Khiew

AUBERGINE WITH LENTILS

125 g (4 oz) lentils
½ teaspoon salt
250 g (8 oz) aubergine (eggplant)
4 cloves garlic
1 fresh chili
2 tablespoons vegetable oil
1 tablespoon fish sauce
4 tablespoons water
10 mint leaves

Cover the lentils with boiling water and leave for 2 hours. Drain, cover with fresh water, add salt, bring to the boil and cook, covered for ½ hour. Drain.

Cut the aubergines lengthways into 4 pieces and then cut these quarters into 5-cm (2-inch) pieces.

Pound the garlic and chili together. Then fry them in the vegetable oil until golden.

Add the lentils, fish sauce, aubergine pieces and water to the garlic and chili in the pan. Continue frying for 2-3 minutes until the aubergine is cooked.

Add the mint leaves, turn the mixture just once with a spoon, and remove from the heat.

Yam Makhua Phao

SWEET AND SOUR AUBERGINES

4 aubergines (eggplants)
3 shallots, chopped
3 tablespoons fish sauce
3 tablespoons lemon juice
1 tablespoon sugar
Garnish:
10 coriander leaves
4 tablespoons powdered dried shrimp

Cook the aubergines whole in a hot oven (230°C/450°F/Gas Mark 8) or barbecue them directly over strong heat until the skins are burnt.

Toss the aubergines into cold water, then peel and dice. Place the pieces in a serving dish and stir in the chopped shallot.

Mix the fish sauce, lemon juice and sugar in a pan and bring to the boil. Pour over the aubergines.

Serve sprinkled with coriander leaves and powdered shrimp. This dish goes well with meat or fish, but can also be served with Plain Rice (Khao Suoy).

Khai Jiew Mangsawirat

VEGETABLE OMELETTE

2 eggs
2-3 tomatoes, chopped
1 small onion, grated
2 tablespoons fish sauce
pepper
3 tablespoons vegetable oil

Beat the eggs together then stir in the tomatoes, onion and fish sauce. Season to taste with pepper.

Heat the oil in a pan until very hot. Pour in the egg mixture and cook until set, tipping the pan and pulling the egg away from the edge as it cooks to allow the uncooked egg to run down and cook. Serve immediately.

Yam Yai

MIXED MEAT SALAD WITH CHINESE VERMICELLI

150 g (5 oz) pork, finely sliced
150 g (5 oz) chicken breast, finely sliced
125 g (4 oz) pig's liver, finely sliced
16 prawns (shrimp), shelled
150 g (5 oz) cuttlefish
10 Chinese mushrooms (optional)
300 g (11 oz) bean thread vermicelli
5 radishes
½ cucumber
1 tomato, quartered
2 hard-boiled eggs, quartered
1 green pepper (capsicum)
coriander sprigs
Dressing:
1 coriander root, crushed
10 coriander leaves
4 cloves garlic, crushed
4 small fresh red chilies, crushed
3 tablespoons sugar
2 tablespoons Japanese soya sauce
3 tablespoons vinegar
2 tablespoons lemon juice
2 tablespoons oil
salt to taste

Simmer the pork, chicken, liver, prawns and cuttlefish in lightly salted water for a few minutes, removing the different ingredients as they become cooked.

Allow to cool, then cut the cuttlefish into pieces and the prawns into halves.

Meanwhile, soak the dried Chinese mushrooms in warm water for 30 minutes, if using. Drain well and quarter. Cut the vermicelli into three. Soak it for 5 minutes in hot water, then drain well. Slice the radishes and cucumber. Halve the tomato and egg quarters, and cut the green pepper into strips. Arrange all the salad ingredients on plates, garnishing with coriander sprigs.

Mix the dressing ingredients together and pour over the salad or serve separately.

Mixed Meat Salad with Chinese Vermicelli shown without its dressing

Scallop Salad

Yam Hoy Shell

SCALLOP SALAD

9 scallops in shells
1 lettuce
1 large onion, finely sliced
5 stems coriander (optional)
Dressing:
2 tablespoons lemon juice
2 cloves garlic, crushed
2 small chilies, crushed
salt
1 tablespoon olive oil
whole chilies to taste

Buy the scallops already opened. Slide them off the flat shells, removing the black beards and intestines. Wash them well, then place them in a saucepan of cold water. Bring to simmering point, skim, and cook gently for 5-10 minutes.

Meanwhile, wash the shells and line them with leaves taken from the heart of the lettuce.

Slice the cooked scallops or leave them whole and arrange them on the lettuce with the onion and the coarsely chopped coriander, if using.

Mix the dressing ingredients together thoroughly, adding as many whole chilies as you like, or none at all if you prefer. One can be made into a flower (page 22) and used for garnishing. Serve the dressing with the scallops, or pour it over them.

Chicken Cabbage Salad

Yam Kalam Pli Sai Kai

CHICKEN CABBAGE SALAD

½ cabbage
300 g (10 oz) cooked chicken breast
2 carrots, grated
1 green pepper (capsicum), cut in thin strips
Dressing:
1 red chili, crushed
2 cloves garlic, crushed
2 tablespoons lemon juice
2 tablespoons dark soya sauce
½ cup (50 g/2 oz) flaked almonds
1 teaspoon salt

Shred the cabbage and plunge it into a pan of boiling water, preferably in a blanching basket, for 1 minute, then transfer it immediately to ice-cold water. Drain and pat dry. Shred the chicken breast.

Arrange the cabbage around the edge of a serving dish then, working towards the centre, arrange a ring of carrots, then peppers, with the chicken filling up the middle of the dish.

Mix the dressing ingredients together and serve with the salad.

Sang Wa Kung

LEMON AND GINGER PRAWN SALAD

Dressing:
1 tablespoon lemon juice
1 tablespoon tamarind juice
2 tablespoons fish sauce
1 teaspoon sugar
Salad:
500 g (1 lb) prawns (shrimp), shelled
5 shallots, finely chopped
2 stalks lemon grass, chopped
2 large red chilies
2 tablespoons grated ginger
2 tablespoons chopped bergamot leaves
Garnish:
mint and basil leaves

Put the lemon juice, tamarind juice, fish sauce and sugar into a small saucepan. Bring to the boil, stirring occasionally. Remove from the heat and leave to cool.

Cook the prawns in boiling water for 2-3 minutes, or place them on aluminium foil and barbecue over medium heat until they turn pink. Leave to cool.

In a serving bowl, mix together the prawns, shallots, lemon grass, whole chilies, ginger and bergamot. Pour the cooled dressing over the salad and stir well.

Serve garnished with the mint and basil leaves.

Yam Nua Phla

BEEF SALAD

850 g (1¾ lb) beef fillet, in a piece
3 cloves garlic, chopped
15 mint leaves
4 small chilies, sliced into rings
2 onions, finely chopped
2 tablespoons lemon juice
2 tablespoons fish sauce
pepper
salt
2-3 lettuce leaves
Garnish:
1 tomato, sliced
2 spring onions (scallions), chopped
3 coriander leaves, chopped

Roast the beef in a hot oven (220°C/425°F/Gas Mark 7) allowing 15 minutes per 500 g (1 lb). Transfer to a rack and leave to cool.

Slice the beef into thin strips, then mix with the garlic, mint, chili, onions, lemon juice, fish sauce and a little pepper and salt.

Serve on a bed of lettuce leaves and garnish with slices of tomato. Sprinkle with the chopped spring onions and coriander leaves.

Sang Wa Pla Muk Sod

CUTTLEFISH SALAD

600 g (1 ¼ lb) cuttlefish
Dressing:
2 tablespoons lemon juice
1 tablespoon fish sauce
1 tablespoon chopped lemon grass stalk
1 tablespoon grated ginger or
1 pinch ground ginger
1 tablespoon chopped shallots
Garnish:
1 tablespoon chopped coriander leaves
1 tablespoon chopped spring onions (scallions)
6 mint leaves
3 chilies, lightly crushed

Wash the cuttlefish carefully, drain and slice thinly.

Half fill a saucepan with water and bring it to simmering point. Place the slices of cuttlefish in a strainer and hold it in the water for 2 minutes. Transfer the cooked cuttlefish to a bowl. Pour the lemon juice and fish sauce over it. Add the lemon grass, ginger and shallots and mix well.

Serve sprinkled with the chopped coriander and spring onions, mint leaves and chilies.

Yam Hoy Malangpoo

MUSSEL SALAD

2 kg (4 ½ lb) mussels
butter for frying
1 tablespoon fish sauce
3 tablespoons lemon juice
3 stalks lemon grass, chopped
1 tablespoon chopped bergamot leaves
3 shallots, chopped
salt
Garnish:
coriander leaves
4 chilies, crushed

Scrape the mussels clean. Discard any that are open. Wash several times and drain.

Heat the mussels with a little butter in a hot frying pan. Remove from the heat when the mussels open and the flesh turns white. Discard those which do not open. Mix the mussels with the fish sauce, lemon juice, lemon grass, bergamot leaves and shallots. Stir well and season with salt to taste.

Serve sprinkled with the coriander leaves and chilies.

Yam Taeng

CUCUMBER SALAD

300 g (10 oz) prawns (shrimp)
350 g (12 oz) cucumber
Dressing:
3 shallots, finely chopped
1 tablespoon lemon juice
2 teaspoons fish sauce
1 small chili, sliced into rings
Garnish:
chopped parsley

Buy the prawns ready-cooked or drop them uncooked into boiling water for 3 minutes then leave them to cool in the liquid.

Peel the cucumber and slice it finely. Shell the prawns and cut them in half lengthways. Place the cucumber and prawns in a salad bowl.

Mix together the shallots, lemon juice, fish sauce and chili. Pour this dressing over the prawn and cucumber slices and stir. Leave to stand for 5 minutes before serving sprinkled with parsley.

Som Tam Malakor

PAPAYA SALAD

4-5 cups coarsely grated unripe papaya
3 cloves garlic, chopped
3 small chilies, chopped
1 tablespoon fish sauce
2 tablespoons lemon juice
2 tablespoons crushed peanuts
pepper to taste
lettuce and cabbage leaves
Garnish:
tomato slices
tomato rose

Mixed the grated papaya with the garlic, chilies, fish sauce, lemon juice and peanuts. Season with pepper.

Serve on a bed of lettuce and cabbage leaves. Garnish with slices of tomato and a tomato rose (page 23).

Phla Kung

PRAWN SALAD WITH LEMON GRASS

800 g (1¾ lb) prawns (shrimp)
Dressing:
3 tablespoons lemon juice
1 tablespoon fish sauce
4 shallots, chopped
15 mint leaves
1 stalk lemon grass, finely chopped
5 lettuce leaves
Garnish:
1 teaspoon chopped coriander leaves
1 teaspoon chopped spring onions (scallions)
1 teaspoon chopped chilies

Buy the prawns ready-cooked or cook them in boiling water for 2-3 minutes, then leave them to cool in the liquid. Shell them and place them in a large bowl.

Mix together the lemon juice, fish sauce, shallots, mint leaves and lemon grass. Pour this dressing over the prawns and stir well.

Line a serving dish with lettuce leaves and pile on the salad. Sprinkle with the chopped coriander leaves, spring onions and chilies.

Papaya Salad (top); Spicy Ground Beef with Mint (recipe page 103).

Yam Thua Fak Yao

FRENCH BEAN SALAD

300 g (10 oz) French beans
salt
4 tablespoons coconut milk
3 shallots, chopped
2 cloves garlic
1 dried chili
3 tablespoons lemon juice
1 tablespoon brown sugar
3 tablespoons fish sauce
¼ cup (25 g/1 oz) preroasted peanuts
Garnish:
1 onion, chopped and fried

Cut the French beans into 5-cm (2-inch) lengths and cook for 3 minutes in boiling salted water. Drain and cool.

Bring the coconut milk to the boil, then leave it to cool.

Dry-fry the shallots and garlic until browned, then pound them together with the chili. Add the lemon juice, sugar and fish sauce, then add this mixture to the French beans. Crush the peanuts coarsely and stir in to the beans with the coconut milk. Garnish with fried onion.

Yam Kalampli

CABBAGE SALAD

¼ cup (25 g/1 oz) grated coconut
500 g (1 lb) cabbage
¼ cup (50 g/2 oz) sliced onion
5 cloves garlic, chopped
1 tablespoon crushed dried chili
4 tablespooons lemon juice
1 teaspoon salt
4 tablespoons fish sauce
1 tablespoon brown sugar
½ cup (75 g/3 oz) preroasted peanuts

Put the grated coconut in a dry pan over low heat and stir constantly until it turns golden brown. Remove from the heat.

Cut the cabbage in half, remove the hard centre and then cut lengthways into 5-mm (¼-inch) thick slices.

Dry-fry the onion and garlic until browned. Pound the onion and garlic with the crushed chili, then add in the lemon juice, salt, fish sauce and sugar. Mix well, then stir in the cabbage.

Crush the peanuts coarsely and add to the cabbage with the grated coconut. Mix well and serve.

Yam Khai Khem

SALTED EGG SALAD

6 salted eggs, boiled (page 35)
2 tablespoons chopped shallots
2 chilies, finely sliced into rings
4 spring onions (scallions), sliced
2 lemons, cut into quarters

Cut the eggs in half and scoop out the yolks. Slice the whites and arrange with the yolks on a serving dish. Sprinkle with the shallots and chilies. Garnish with spring onions and lemon quarters.

Squeeze the juice from the lemon quarters over the eggs before eating.

Serve with Plain Rice (Khao Suoy) or Rice Soup (Khao Tom Kai).

Miang Pla Tou

SPICY MACKEREL SALAD

4 medium mackerel
oil for frying
4-5 shallots, chopped
1 tablespoon grated ginger
4 small red chilies, crushed
4 small green chilies
3 tablespoons crushed peanuts
½ green apple, cut into fine strips
3 tablespoons lemon juice
1 tablespoon grated lemon rind
salt
black pepper, freshly ground
5 lettuce leaves
Garnish:
coriander leaves

Wash and gut the fish and steam for 5-7 minutes. Before they are completely cooked remove the fish from the steamer and dry them.

Fry the steamed fish on both sides in the hot oil until golden. Remove the bones and skin, and flake the flesh.

In a bowl, mix the fish meat with the shallots, ginger, chilies, peanuts and apple. Add the lemon juice and rind. Season with salt and pepper to taste. Mix well.

Serve on the bed of lettuce leaves, and sprinkle with coriander leaves.

Som Tam Kalam Pli

CABBAGE AND NUT SALAD

½ white cabbage, shredded
2 tomatoes, diced
2 carrots, grated
2 tablespoons lemon juice
½ teaspoon grated lemon rind
1 clove garlic, finely chopped
salt
pepper
Garnish:
1 tablespoon crushed almonds or peanuts

Mix the cabbage, tomatoes and carrot in a salad bowl.

Stir in the lemon juice and rind, garlic, salt and pepper. Serve sprinkled with the nuts.

Yam Hed

MUSHROOM SALAD

300 g (10 oz) mushrooms
1 head celery
1 spring onion (scallion)
2 tablespoons grated onion
3 tablespoons lemon juice
1 tablespoon fish sauce
½ teaspoon salt
½ teaspoon sugar
½ teaspoon chopped fresh chili
½ cup mint leaves
To serve:
1 small lettuce

Cut the mushrooms into quarters. Bring a pan of water to the boil. Remove the water from the heat. Add the mushrooms and leave for 3 minutes. Drain.

Cut the celery and spring onion into 1-cm (½-inch) pieces.

Mix the mushrooms, onion, spring onion and celery together, then stir in the lemon juice, fish sauce, salt, sugar, chili and mint leaves.

Serve on a bed of lettuce leaves.

Meat and Poultry

Meat and Poultry

Until the middle of the 19th century, the Thais ate with their hands, like the Indians and Burmese. For soup, they used spoons made of porcelain or mother-of-pearl. Later, forks were introduced, but knives have always remained in the kitchen. That is one of the reasons why meat, fish and vegetables are usually served in small pieces. Learning how to cut food up properly is therefore essential. Every Thai kitchen contains a solid chopping board, a chopper, a sharp butcher's knife and a small pointed knife. The dexterity with which Thai cooks use these implements reveals a true art, as they shred, slice, carve and chop with nonchalant ease. For some curries, the meat is cut into larger pieces than for other dishes. Poultry is cut up in much the same way as in the West; the legs and wings are removed first, then the breast is sliced lengthways, before being cut into bite-sized morsels. For sautéed dishes, both meat and poultry are reduced to pieces which, when combined with a little rice, are the size of one mouthful. Sometimes, a bird is cooked whole, for example Peking duck or flambéed chicken, and cut up before being served.

In any case, the quantity of meat eaten is fairly small. Killing animals does not lie easily on a Buddhist conscience, and the sight of a Thai butcher is rare. This job is left to the Chinese, who specialize in pork, and to the Muslims, who deal with beef, mutton and chicken. These days, poultry is often sold in pieces. Meat is set out on stalls in the open-air. Thais distrust frozen meat which is not widely available anyway, and do not mind going to market twice a day.

Chicken is the most popular sort of poultry as it is relatively cheap, its bland flavour goes well with a variety of spices and sauces, it is useful in making a stock base for soups and, as the song says, "everything's good in a chicken". The poor and rich alike eat chicken. Thailand has a modern poultry industry alongside family farm production; country roads are full of chickens scratching for grain. Chicken can be skewered and grilled over charcoal, or sautéed with spices and vegetables. Street vendors sell it grilled, and a choice leg makes an excellent snack to eat whilst going "pai thiaw" (strolling around).

Duck breeding is an increasingly common sight along rivers and canals. The Chinese are particularly keen on this bird, and Peking duck is a gastronomic delicacy. The whole bird is eaten, from the delicately roasted skin cut into strips, to the stock made from the carcass.

In the north, people enjoy sparrows and pigeons, especially when fried with spices.

The choice of meat varies according to religious beliefs and habits; Muslims refuse to touch the pork that the Chinese like so much; the Indians cannot bear the idea of eating beef; the Thais generally hate the smell of mutton. Buffalo is popular in country areas, and can be tenderized by suitable cooking. Veal is rarely found in Thailand. Meat is usually well done and, except when dried, is accompanied by vegetables and spices. Certain restaurants specialize in game, such as vension and wild boar. In memory of harder times it is not unusual to find protein in the form of insects, rodents and reptiles but recipes for cricket, field mouse, snake and lizard are not included in this book!

Larp Nua

SPICY GROUND BEEF WITH MINT

500 g (1 lb) beef, minced or ground
2 cloves garlic, chopped
1 red chili, chopped
1 tablespoon chopped shallot
1 teaspoon fish sauce
2 tablespoons lemon juice
1 teaspoon ground coriander
1 tablespoon golden rice semolina (page 35)
2 tablespoons chopped spring onions (scallions)
salt
mint leaves
lettuce or white cabbage leaves

Fry the beef in a frying pan, without oil, until browned and cooked through. Leave to cool.

Lightly brown the garlic, chili and shallot in a pan over medium heat, again without oil. Pound them together then mix this paste with the meat. Stir in the fish sauce, lemon juice, coriander, rice semolina and spring onions. Season with salt to taste.

Garnish with mint leaves and serve on a bed of lettuce or white cabbage accompanied by raw vegetables of your choice.

Nua Dad Diao

SALTED SUN-DRIED BEEF

4-5 medium steaks
pepper
2 tablespoons light soya sauce
1 teaspoon chopped garlic

Season the steak with pepper and marinate in the soya sauce mixed with the garlic for 10-15 minutes. Place the meat on a grilling tray and leave in the sun for 2 hours.

Cook the meat over a barbecue or under a medium grill according to taste — rare, medium or well done.

Cut the steaks into thin strips and serve with Plain Rice (Khao Suoy) or Coconut Rice (Khao Man).

Mou Wan

CARAMEL PORK

1 onion, sliced
1 tablespoon oil
3 tablespoons sugar
2 tablespoons sweet soya sauce
2 tablespoons fish sauce
400 g (14 oz) pork, cut into thin strips
salt
pepper
1 cup (250 ml/8 fl oz) water

Brown the onion in the oil in a saucepan. Add the sugar, soya sauce, fish sauce, pork, salt and pepper. Stir well then add the water.

Bring the liquid to the boil then reduce the heat to medium.

Stirring occasionally, simmer for about 1 hour or until the pork is tender and the liquid has reduced.

A little more water can be added during cooking if necessary to prevent burning but the dish should be served quite dry.

Luk Chin

MEATBALLS

600 g (1 ¼ lb) beef or pork
4 cloves garlic, crushed
pepper
1 tablespoon flour
1 tablespoon light soya sauce
salt

Mince the meat twice, so that it is as fine as possible, then mix it with the garlic and pepper.

Knead this mixture with the flour and soya sauce, then form into balls.

Bring a pan of lightly salted water to the boil, then throw in the meatballs.

When the meatballs rise to the surface, they are cooked. Remove from the water and drain.

Meatballs are a popular component of many Thai dishes. They are used in soups and curries as well as grilled or fried with salted or sweet and sour sauces.

Caramel Pork with Boiled Eggs

Mou Phalo

CARAMEL PORK WITH BOILED EGGS

5 cloves garlic
8 peppercorns
2 coriander roots
1 tablespoon oil
2 tablespoons sweet soya sauce
2 tablespoons sugar
500 g (1 lb) pork, cut into pieces
3 cups (750 ml/1¼ pints) water
4-6 hard-boiled eggs, shelled

Pound the garlic, peppercorns and coriander roots together then lightly brown this mixture in the oil.

Add the soya sauce and sugar. Lower the heat, and stir with a wooden spoon until the mixture caramelizes.

Add the pork and brown in the caramel mixture.

Pour in the water and when the liquid begins to boil, lower the heat, add the eggs and simmer for about 1 hour, adding more water if necessary.

Halve the eggs before serving the dish with Plain Rice (Khao Suoy).

Beef Sautéed with Pepper

Nua Phad Prik

BEEF SAUTÉED WITH PEPPER

1 clove garlic
4 small red chilies
2 shallots, sliced
2 tablespoons oil
1 green pepper (capsicum), cut into strips
1 tablespoon light soya sauce
2 teaspoons oyster sauce
500 g (1 lb) beef fillet, cut into thin slices
salt
freshly ground black pepper

Chop the garlic and chilies together, then mix with the shallots. Fry this mixture in the hot oil until browned. Add the green pepper and sauté for 3 minutes.

Lower the heat. Add the soya sauce, oyster sauce, meat, salt and pepper. Stir-fry for 1-2 minutes. Serve with Plain Rice (Khao Suoy).

Issan Ground Pork

Lab Mou

ISSAN GROUND PORK

3 shallots
3 cloves garlic
500 g (1 lb) pork, minced or ground
2-3 tablespoons water
3 tablespoons golden rice semolina (page 35)
1 teaspoon salt
3 tablespoons lemon juice
1 tablespoon fish sauce
6 mint leaves
1 tablespoon crushed garlic
2 tablespoons chopped shallot
lettuce leaves
1 tablespoon chopped spring onions (scallions)
1/2 teaspoon chili powder (optional)

Brown the whole shallots and garlic cloves on foil over direct heat. Pound them together and keep to one side.

Boil the pork in the water for 10 minutes, stirring occasionally.

Transfer the meat to a large dish, then stir in the browned and crushed shallots and garlic together with the golden rice semolina, salt, lemon juice and fish sauce. Mix well before adding half the mint leaves, chopped, the crushed garlic and chopped shallot. Fold these last ingredients in gently.

Serve warm on a bed of lettuce. Sprinkle with chopped spring onions, the remaining mint leaves, and chili powder, if liked. Spring onions and cabbage often accompany this dish.

Nua Phad Horapha Krob

SAUTÉED BEEF WITH CRISPY BASIL

3 cloves garlic, pounded
4 small red chilies, crushed
2 tablespoons fish sauce
salt
freshly ground black pepper
500 g (1 lb) beef fillet, cut into thin strips
1 cup basil leaves
1 cup (250 ml/8 fl oz) oil

Mix together the garlic, chilies, fish sauce, salt and black pepper, then marinate the beef in this mixture for 5 minutes.

Fry the basil leaves in the oil until they become transparent. Drain and put to one side.

Remove most of the oil, leaving about 3 tablespoons in the pan. Turn up the heat, add the meat and stir-fry for 2-3 minutes.

When the meat is almost cooked, stir in half the fried basil leaves. Remove from heat immediately and sprinkle the meat with the remaining basil leaves. Serve with Plain Rice (Khao Suoy).

Nua Phad Khing

SAUTÉED VEAL WITH GINGER

6 cloves garlic, chopped
1 tablespoon fermented soya beans
2 tablespoons oil
500 g (1 lb) veal, cut into thin strips
1 tablespoon fish sauce
1 teaspoon sugar
3 tablespoons grated ginger
salt
Garnish:
pepper
10 coriander leaves
2 chilies

Brown the garlic with the soya beans in the oil over medium heat. Add the veal and sauté for 2-3 minutes.

Add the fish sauce, sugar and ginger. Mix well and cook for a 5-6 minutes. Season with salt to taste.

Serve hot, sprinkling with pepper, coriander leaves and chilies.

Sen Mee Nua Yang

GRILLED BEEF WITH RICE VERMICELLI

2 chilies
2 teaspoons finely chopped lemon grass
1 teaspoon salt
500 g (1 lb) beef fillet, sliced
500 g (1 lb) rice vermicelli
4 tablespoons coarsely pounded peanuts
Garnish:
sprigs of fresh mint and basil

Pound together the chilies, lemon grass and salt. Roll the beef in this mixture, and leave for 15 minutes.

Soak the vermicelli in hot water for 5-10 minutes. Drain and put to one side.

Place the beef slices over a barbecue or under a hot grill until cooked according to taste – rare, medium or well done.

Divide the vermicelli into 4-6 portions, and arrange on individual plates.

Cut the beef into slivers. Place about 10 slivers on each portion of vermicelli. Sprinkle with the peanuts. Garnish with the sprigs of mint and basil. Serve with Sweet and Sour Sauce with Turnip and Carrot (Nam Jim Carot).

Kai Ob Klua

SALT-BAKED CHICKEN

1 medium chicken
1 tablespoon coarse salt
1 teaspoon pepper
1 stick celery, chopped
2 small chilies, chopped
1 leek, chopped
4 cloves garlic, chopped
1 teaspoon light soya sauce
1 teaspoon fine salt
1 tablespoon oil
Garnish:
1 sprig coriander

Wash and dry the chicken, and coat the inside with the coarse salt and pepper. Mix together the chopped celery, chilies, leek and garlic and use this mixture to stuff the chicken. Truss the chicken then coat the outside with the soya sauce and fine salt.

Wrap in aluminium foil, and cook in a moderately hot oven (200°C/400°F/Gas Mark 6) allowing 20 minutes per 500 g (1 lb) and 10 minutes over. Remove the foil and rub the chicken with the oil. Return it to a very hot oven (240°C/475°F/Gas Mark 9) for a few minutes to brown.

Carve the chicken, and serve on a dish garnished with the coriander.

Pik Kai Chao Daeng

CHICKEN WINGS IN RICE WINE

1 tablespoon sweet soya sauce
2 tablespoons Maggi sauce
½ cup (125 ml/4 fl oz) rice wine
500 g (1 lb) chicken wings
2 tablespoons oil
10 thin slices fresh ginger
salt
pepper
Garnish:
coriander leaves
2 red chilies, cut into strips or flowers

Mix the soya sauce, Maggi sauce and rice wine together and marinate the chicken wings in this mixture for 15 minutes, then drain.

Heat the oil in a frying pan and add the chicken wings. When the wings are golden brown, place them in a saucepan with enough water to cover. Toss in the slices of ginger. Bring to the boil, then lower the heat and simmer for 30 minutes, adding salt and pepper to taste.

Serve sprinkled with the coriander leaves and red chilies.

Coconut Chicken Curry

Kaeng Khiaw Wan Kai

COCONUT CHICKEN CURRY

2 teaspoons green curry paste (page 43)
1 tablespoon oil
2 cups (450 ml/¾ pint) coconut cream
800 g (1¾ lb) boneless chicken pieces
1 tablespoon light soya sauce
1 aubergine (eggplant), diced
4 red chilies, roughly chopped
5 bergamot leaves
10 basil leaves

Fry the curry paste in the oil. Add half of the coconut cream. When the mixture produces an aroma add the chicken.

Gradually pour in the rest of the coconut cream, stirring constantly. Simmer until the chicken is cooked, about 30 minutes.

Add the soya sauce and the aubergine and bring to simmering point. Stir in the chilies, bergamot and basil. Remove from the heat.

Serve with Plain Rice (Khao Suoy). Tropical fruit such as diced bananas and pineapple is also sometimes served with this dish.

The Thais also sometimes add a small, round, crunchy vegetable which is popular there but not well-known internationally.

Flambéed Chicken with a garnish of green vegetable and tomato roses.

Stuffed Chicken Wings

Masaman Chicken Curry

Kai Lui Fai

FLAMBÉED CHICKEN

1 medium chicken, cleaned and drained
1 stick cinnamon
4 cloves garlic
2 coriander roots
1 star anise pod
2 thin slices galangal
1 tablespoon light soya sauce
1 tablespoon dark soya sauce
1 teaspoon sugar
1 teaspoon pepper
oil for frying
3 tablespoons rum

Place the chicken in a large pan with enough water to cover it, then add the other ingredients except the oil and rum.

Bring to the boil, cover and simmer for ¾-1 hour over low heat. Remove from the heat. Take out the chicken and drain it well.

Heat the oil in a frying pan. Brown the chicken in the oil, turning the bird frequently to ensure that it colours evenly on all sides. Remove and drain.

Shape a sheet of aluminium foil into a basket or bird and place the chicken in it. Pour the rum over the chicken and set light to it in front of the diners. Serve with Red Sauce (Sauce Nam Daeng).

Pik Kai Yad Sai

STUFFED CHICKEN WINGS

8-12 chicken wings
5 coriander roots, chopped
10 peppercorns
3 cloves garlic
400 g (14 oz) pork, minced or ground
2 tablespoons light soya sauce
1 cup (250 ml/8 fl oz) oil
a few coriander leaves
2 tablespoons chili sauce
3 tablespoons tomato sauce
1 tablespoon sugar
Garnish:
5 lettuce leaves
2 tomatoes

Remove the bones from the chicken wings leaving the tips intact and without tearing the skin.

Pound together the coriander, peppercorns and garlic. Mix in the pork and sprinkle with a little of the soya sauce.

Stuff the chicken wings with the pork mixture and fry them in the oil over medium heat until golden, sprinkling with the coriander leaves.

To make the sauce, remove the oil from the pan and pour in the chili sauce, tomato sauce, sugar and the remaining soya sauce. Bring to the boil and simmer for 2 minutes. (If you do not have any of the chili or tomato sauces on pages 40 and 41 already made, the bottled varieties will do.)

Serve the chicken wings on a bed of lettuce, garnished with tomatoes and accompanied by the sauce in small bowls.

Kaeng Masaman Kai

MASAMAN CHICKEN CURRY

4 cups (1 litre/1¾ pints) coconut cream
1 kg (2 lb) chicken pieces
3 potatoes, peeled and quartered
1 onion, halved
½ cup (125 g/4 oz) peanuts
2 teaspoons salt
3 tablespoons masaman curry paste (page 43)
3 tablespoons fish sauce
1 tablespoon tamarind juice
1 tablespoon sugar

Bring the coconut cream to the boil in a large saucepan.

Add the chicken, potatoes, onion, peanuts and salt, and simmer for 20 minutes.

Remove a ladleful of coconut cream from the pan, and pour it into a frying pan. Add the masaman curry paste. Stir until the mixture thickens.

Pour the curry over the chicken. Add the fish sauce, tamarind juice and sugar and stir well. Simmer for a further 15 minutes.

Serve with Plain Rice (Khao Suoy) or bread. Cucumber Sauce (Ajad) is also a popular accompaniment.

Ped Ob Manao

ROAST DUCK WITH LEMON

1 medium duck
1 teaspoon pepper
1 teaspoon salt
2 tablespoons sweet soya sauce
Sauce:
2 tablespoons sugar
1 teaspoon salt
1 tablespoon lemon juice
2 teaspoons flour
1 cup (250 ml/8 fl oz) water
Garnish:
2 lemons, sliced into thin rings
2 tomatoes, sliced into rings

Clean and dry the duck. Season the inside with half the salt and pepper. Coat the outside with the soya sauce and the remaining salt and pepper.

Roast in a hot oven (220°C/425°F/Gas Mark 7) allowing 20 minutes per 500 g (1 lb). When golden brown, remove from the oven and place on a serving dish.

Meanwhile, mix all the sauce ingredients together in a pan. Bring to the boil, stirring constantly, until the sauce thickens.

Pour the sauce over the duck just before serving, garnished with lemon and tomato slices.

Ped Lon

FIVE FLAVOUR DUCK

1 medium duck
oil for frying
1 tablespoon sweet soya sauce
1 tablespoon light soya sauce
3 cloves cardamom
10 thin slices ginger
3 thin slices galangal
1 stick cinnamon
3 star anise pods
2 tablespoons rice wine
¼ green cabbbage, cut into thin strips

Clean out the duck, wash it and let it drain. Place it in a large frying pan with a little hot oil over medium heat. Turn it over several times until browned on all sides. Transfer the duck to a large saucepan with enough water to cover, then add the sweet soya sauce, the light soya sauce, cardamom, ginger, galangal, cinnamon, anise and rice wine. Bring to the boil and simmer for 3 hours.

Remove the duck from the pan, dry it and fry it in fresh oil until the skin is crispy. Remove the duck and fry the cabbage in the same oil.

Serve the duck with the fried cabbage. Have a bowl of soya sauce on the side.

Kaeng Phed Ped Yang

DUCK WITH CURRY

1 medium-sized roast duck
3 cups (750 ml/1¼ pints) coconut cream
½ cup (125 ml/4 fl oz) water
2-3 tablespoons red curry paste (page 42)
10 bergamot leaves
3 tablespoons fish sauce
½ cup (75 g/3 oz) frozen peas
5 small tomatoes, halved
4 red or green chilies, cut into strips
10 basil leaves

Remove the duck meat from the bones and cut it into bite-sized pieces.

In a small pan, bring half the coconut cream to the boil with the water. Leave to simmer.

In another pan, bring to the boil a third of the remaining coconut cream, then stir in the curry paste. Cook for a few minutes before adding the bergamot and the pieces of duck. Stir well.

Add the simmering coconut cream and turn up the heat.

Add the fish sauce, peas, tomatoes and chilies. Simmer until the peas are cooked then add the rest of the coconut cream and bring to the boil.

Sprinkle with the basil leaves and remove from the heat. Serve with Plain Rice (Khao Suoy).

The Thais also sometimes add a small, round, crunchy vegetable which is popular there but not well-known internationally.

Duck with Curry

Kai Phalo

CARAMEL CHICKEN WITH BOILED EGGS

2 cloves garlic, chopped
1 teaspoon chopped coriander root
oil for frying
6 chicken drumsticks
2 tablespoons sweet soya sauce
1 teaspoon sugar
1 teaspoon salt
2 cups (450 ml/³/₄ pint) water
6 hard-boiled eggs, shelled
½ teaspoon ground cinnamon

Brown the garlic and coriander in the oil. Add the chicken and brown on all sides.

Add the soya sauce, sugar and salt. Lower the heat and stir until the mixture caramelizes slightly. Add the water and eggs, and sprinkle with cinnamon.

Increase the heat to bring the mixture to the boil, then lower the heat again and simmer for 40 minutes until the chicken is cooked and the sauce has reduced. Cut the eggs into quarters before serving.

Yam Kai Prik Wan

SPICY CHOPPED CHICKEN

300 g (10 oz) cooked chicken breast
2 shallots, chopped
3 spring onions (scallions), chopped
1 green pepper (capsicum), sliced into rings
2 tablespoons lemon juice
1 tablespoon light soya sauce
1 pinch chili powder
Garnish:
10 mint leaves
5 coriander leaves

Chop the chicken breast then mix together all the ingredients except the garnish. Sprinkle with the chopped mint and coriander leaves. Serve with Plain Rice (Khao Suoy).

Kaeng Phanang Kai Thung Tua

WHOLE CHICKEN WITH PHANANG CURRY

1 medium chicken, cleaned and drained
2 cups (450 ml/³/₄ pint) water
3 cups (750 ml/1¼ pints) coconut cream
2 tablespoons phanang curry paste (page 43)
4 tablespoons fish sauce
1 tablespoon sugar
Garnish:
6 basil leaves
3 red chilies, cut into strips or flowers

Boil the chicken whole, in the water with a third of the coconut cream for about 1 hour until almost all the liquid has evaporated and the chicken is tender.

In a small saucepan, simmer the rest of the coconut cream over medium heat.

Measure 4 tablespoons boiling coconut cream into a frying pan. Add the curry paste and cook for 3 minutes. Pour this sauce over the chicken. Add the remaining coconut cream, fish sauce and sugar. Cook until the sauce thickens, then remove from the heat.

Serve the chicken in its sauce garnished with the basil leaves and chilies.

Kai Yang Khing

ISSAN ROAST CHICKEN

4 cloves garlic
1 slice fresh ginger
1 teaspoon ground coriander
pepper
salt
1 tablespoon vegetable oil
1 medium chicken, jointed

Pound the garlic, ginger, coriander, pepper and salt together. Add the oil and mix well.

Marinate the chicken joints in this mixture for 1-2 hours.

Roast the chicken in a moderate oven, (180°C/350°F/Gas Mark 4) for 20 minutes, turning the pieces from time to time.

Kai Phad Kaprao

CHICKEN SAUTÉED WITH BASIL

5 cloves garlic, crushed
½ cup (125 ml/4 fl oz) oil
4 small chilies, crushed
500 g (1 lb) chicken breast, diced
1 tablespoon fish sauce
1 tablespoon light soya sauce
pepper
20 basil leaves

Brown the garlic in the oil. Add the chilies and the chicken. Increase the heat to sauté the chicken, then turn down the heat, cover and cook for few minutes until the chicken is cooked through. Stir occasionally to prevent the meat from sticking to the pan.

Add the fish sauce, soya sauce and pepper and stir well.

Toss in the basil leaves. Cover for 2 minutes. Stir and remove from the heat.

Kai Daeng

RED CHICKEN

½ cup (125 ml/4 fl oz) coconut milk
¾ cup (175 ml/6 fl oz) water
600 g (1¼ lb) chicken breast, finely sliced
2 tablespoons red curry paste (page 42)
1 large sugar cube
2 tablespoons fish sauce
15 basil leaves
3 bergamot leaves, finely chopped
3 large red chilies, sliced into strips

Bring half the coconut milk to the boil with the water.

When the mixture boils, stir in the chicken and simmer for 8-10 minutes or until the chicken is cooked. Carefully stir in the curry paste, sugar and fish sauce. Mix well, then sprinkle with the basil and bergamot leaves and the chili. Just before serving, pour the remaining coconut milk over the dish. Serve with hot Plain Rice (Khao Suoy).

Kaeng Kai

CHICKEN CURRY WITH SOUR CREAM

800 g (1¾ lb) chicken pieces
oil for frying
5 bergamot leaves
2 teaspoons green curry paste (page 43)
2 cups (450 ml/¾ pint) chicken stock (page 34)
1 aubergine (eggplant), diced
2 small chilies
10 basil leaves
½ cup (125 ml/4 fl oz) sour cream

Brown the chicken in the oil, over medium heat. Add the bergamot and cook for 2 more minutes.

Remove the chicken, and fry the curry paste in the same oil.

When a strong aroma is produced, return the chicken to the pan. Gradually add the stock, followed by the aubergine. Cover, and simmer for 30-40 minutes or until the chicken is cooked. Add the chilies and the basil. Simmer for a further 2 minutes.

Remove the chilies. Add the sour cream and stir in well without boiling. Cover and remove from the heat.

Serve with Plain Rice (Khao Suoy).

Vegetarian Dishes

Now fashionable in the West, there is, however, nothing new about vegetarian cooking. It has been a traditional element of Asian religions for over two thousand years. It is also linked to the age-old virtues of herbal remedies which are the basis of traditional medicine.

Doing without meat is both a way of respecting the Creator and a means of increasing the vital energy in each individual. Since time immemorial philosophers, yogis, Zen Buddhists and the Buddha himself have taught that killing or destroying life is an insult to the Creation.

The concept of vegetarianism is thus natural and normal in a country as profoundly Buddhist as Thailand, even if it is not always strictly adhered to. One of the fundamental principles of Buddhism is to spare animal life. The killing of living creatures can only have negative consequences. The Thais clear their consciences by getting the Chinese or the Muslims to perform this impure act, but eating meat still involves the taking of life, and our bodies thereby lose some of their vital force.

The last episode of the Buddha's life teaches this lesson very clearly. He generally abstained from meat, and only accepted it to avoid insulting the alms-giver. One day, as he was about to eat what was to be his last meal, his host offered him some pork. The Buddha at first refused, but when the host insisted, he realized that the man was acting with good intentions and accepted. He fell ill after this meal and died.

Each week, on a day determined by the lunar calendar, the faithful go to the temple to gain merit. They offer gifts and food to the monks. The most pious of them imitate the monks that day by eating nothing after noon. Many also abstain from meat. Some Thais follow this diet of rice and vegetables every day.

The current governor of Bangkok has recently been actively encouraging the development of vegetarianism by supporting a Buddhist community called Santi Asoke, which calls for the return to a simple life and for less superstition.

Similarly, a Buddhist monk, the Bhikku Buddhasa, has just published a book on vegetarian cooking in which he suggests that readers try a vegetables-only diet for three months to see if this improves their intellectual and spiritual life. Vegetarianism is, indeed, reputed to preserve sensory perception and quick-wittedness, and we are frequently advised these days of the benefits to the health of eating more vegetables and less animal products. However there is no question of accepting these ideas blindly. The Buddha himself taught that the validity of any doctrine should be tested through personal experience.

If you are interested in vegetarian cooking, why not try the Thai variety? You don't have to make a total commitment. These dishes make interesting and unusual additions to any meal, and will probably be most useful to those people who want to reduce the proportion of meat in their diets but have problems finding enough appetizing ways to prepare and serve vegetables.

Masaman Mangsawirat

VEGETARIAN CURRY

3 medium potatoes
5 shallots, sliced
1 tablespoon sliced lemon grass
½ teaspoon sliced galangal
2 cloves
1 tablespoon coriander seeds
1 teaspoon cummin seeds
5 dried chilies
1 teaspoon salt
10 cloves garlic
3 peppercorns
½ teaspoon ground cinnamon
4 cups (1 litre/1¾ pints) coconut milk
3 medium squares hard beancurd
4 tablespoons preroasted peanuts
5 cardamom seeds, roasted
3 onions, halved
2 tablespoons brown sugar
3 tablespoons light soya sauce
3 tablespoons vinegar
3 tablespoons tamarind juice

Par-boil, peel and dice the potatoes. Meanwhile dry-fry the shallots, lemon grass and galangal in one pan until browned, and dry-fry the cloves, coriander seeds and cummin in another pan until they look and smell roasted. Soak the dried chilies in hot water for 10 minutes.

Pound together the chilies, salt, lemon grass, galangal, shallots, garlic, cloves, coriander seeds, cummin, peppercorns and ground cinnamon.

Heat the coconut milk until warm and stir in the pounded ingredients.

Cut the beancurd into small cubes and add it to the coconut milk mixture with the peanuts, cardamom seeds, potatoes, halved onions, brown sugar, light soya sauce, vinegar and tamarind juice.

Simmer for 30 minutes, stirring from time to time.

Con Tao Jiaw Sai Thua

BEANS WITH EGG SAUCE

½ cup (125 g/4 oz) canned soya beans
¼ cup (50 g/2 oz) fermented soya beans
2 cups (450 ml/¾ pint) coconut milk
1 tablespoon brown sugar
2 tablespoons tamarind juice
2 fresh chilies, sliced
3 shallots, sliced
1 egg, beaten

Pound together the drained canned soya beans and the fermented soya beans.

Heat the coconut milk until warm and then stir in the pounded beans.

Add the sugar, tamarind juice, chilies and shallots to the coconut milk and bean mixture.

Finally, add the egg and stir all ingredients together. Bring to simmering point, stirring. Simmer for 3-5 minutes before serving with fresh vegetables such as cucumbers, Chinese cabbage and lettuce.

Yam Nam Sod

VERMICELLI SALAD WITH GINGER

125 g (4 oz) rice vermicelli
2 spring onions (scallions)
4 tablespoons grated ginger
4 tablespoons chopped shallots
2 tablespoons soya sauce
2 tablespoons lemon juice
½ cup (75 g/3 oz) peanuts
Garnish:
15 coriander leaves
2 small chilies, chopped

Soak the vermicelli in lukewarm water for 10 minutes. Drain, cool and cut up. Cut the spring onions into pieces and mix with the vermicelli. Add the ginger, shallots, soya sauce, lemon juice and coarsely crushed peanuts.

Serve on a plate, sprinkled with coriander and chili.

Sweet and Sour Vegetables

Phad Phak Priew Wan

SWEET AND SOUR VEGETABLES

½ cucumber
½ pineapple, peeled
1 medium square hard beancurd
1 green pepper (capsicum), optional
3 cloves garlic, pounded
3 tablespoons vegetable oil
1 large onion, sliced
1-2 tomatoes, quartered
1 tablespoon light soya sauce
1 teaspoon salt
1 teaspoon brown sugar

Cut the cucumber lengthways into 4 pieces and then cut the 4 long pieces into 5-cm (2-inch) pieces.

Dice the pineapple, cut the beancurd into small pieces and the green pepper into strips.

Fry the garlic in the oil until it is browned. Add the onion and beancurd and continue frying until the onion is tender.

Add the pineapple, cucumber, tomato, soya sauce, salt, sugar and green pepper, if using, to the pan, and fry with the other ingredients for 2-3 minutes. If the mixture becomes too dry, add a little water.

Serve immediately.

Beancurd and Celery

Tao Hou Phad Khuen Thai

BEANCURD AND CELERY

1 head celery
2 medium squares soft beancurd
2 cloves garlic, chopped
1 tablespoon vegetable oil
1 tablespoon fermented soya beans
1 teaspoon light soya sauce

Cut the celery into 2.5-cm (1-inch) lengths. If you are using Thai celery, leave it in long sticks. Slice the beancurd.

Fry the garlic in the oil until browned and then add the fermented soya beans, soya sauce and celery. Continue frying for no more than 5 minutes.

Add the beancurd to the pan and fry for a further 2 minutes. Remove from the heat and serve.

Carb Thua Daeng

KIDNEY BEAN SALAD

½ teaspoon chili powder
1 tablespoon chopped shallots
1 tablespoon crushed garlic
1 teaspoon chopped galangal
1 teaspoon finely sliced lemon grass
1 teaspoon salt
2 tablespoons vegetable oil
½ piece hard beancurd
1 cup (300 g/10 oz) canned kidney beans
3 tablespoons vegetable stock (page 34)
1 tablespoon lemon juice
1 tablespoon light soya sauce
To serve:
1 lettuce
1 Chinese cabbage
1 tablespoon chopped coriander leaves
1 tablespoon chopped mint leaves
1 cucumber, sliced

Pound together the chili, shallots, garlic, galangal, lemon grass and salt.

Fry the pounded ingredients in the vegetable oil. Cut the beancurd into matchsticks and add to the pan with the drained kidney beans and stock. Keep frying until the liquid has reduced and the mixture is dry.

Remove from the heat. Add the lemon juice and soya sauce and mix well. Allow to cool.

When cold serve the kidney bean mixture on a thick bed of lettuce and cabbage leaves. Garnish with coriander, mint and cucumber.

Hor Mok Nor Mai

BAMBOO SHOOTS IN SAUCE

500 g (1 lb) bamboo shoots
3 dried chilies
2 cups (450 ml/¾ pint) coconut milk
1 tablespoon rice flour
1 teaspoon salt
5 shallots, chopped
7 cloves garlic
1 teaspoon chopped galangal
1 tablespoon chopped lemon grass
1 teaspoon chopped bergamot skin
2 teaspoons chopped coriander root
5 peppercorns
2 tablespoons light soya sauce
10 basil leaves
Garnish:
10 coriander leaves, chopped
1 fresh chili, sliced in rounds

If using fresh bamboo shoots, peel off the tough skin, then simmer the shoots in a little water for 30 minutes. The canned variety should be simmered in water for 10 minutes. Drain, and when cool, shred or grate the shoots. Soak the dried chilies in hot water for 10 minutes.

Heat the coconut milk until it is warm and then add the flour and salt.

Pound together the dried chilies, shallots, garlic, galangal, lemon grass, bergamot skin, coriander root and peppercorns. Then add this mixture to the coconut milk.

Stir in the grated bamboo shoots together with the soya sauce and basil leaves. Return to simmering point, stirring, then pour the mixture into a dish. Garnish with coriander leaves and fresh chili. Place in a steamer over boiling water and steam for 10 minutes.

Khao Phad Thua Sai Khai

FRIED RICE WITH BEANS AND EGG

½ cup (125 g/4 oz) white or haricot beans
½ teaspoon salt
2 cloves garlic, crushed
2 tablespoons vegetable oil
4 cups (750 g/1½ lb) cooked plain rice (page 32)
2 tablespoons light soya sauce
1 egg
1 cucumber, sliced

Soak the beans in cold water overnight. Drain, then cover with fresh water. Add salt, bring to the boil and simmer for 1 hour. Drain.

Fry the garlic in the vegetable oil until browned, then add the beans, rice and light soya sauce. Fry for 3-5 minutes.

Push the rice to the sides of the pan, crack open the egg, and pour it into the centre of the pan. Cover the egg with the rice mixture. Continue frying for a further 3-5 minutes.

Serve with the sliced cucumber.

Khao Phad Khamin

TURMERIC FRIED RICE

4 cloves garlic, chopped
4 tablespoons vegetable oil
1 onion, sliced
1 cup (150 g/5 oz) diced pumpkin
4 cups (750 g/1½ lb) cooked plain rice (page 32)
125 g (4 oz) mushrooms, sliced
250 g (8 oz) tomatoes, chopped
1 teaspoon brown sugar
3 tablespoons light soya sauce
¼ tablespoon curry powder
½ tablespoon turmeric powder
¼ teaspoon pepper
125 g (4 oz) spring onions (scallions)

Fry the garlic in the oil until browned. Then add the onion and pumpkin. Fry for 2-3 minutes.

Add the rice, mushrooms, tomatoes, brown sugar and light soya sauce. Continue frying for another 2-3 minutes.

Then add the curry powder, turmeric powder and pepper. Mix well with the other ingredients.

Cut the spring onions into pieces and sprinkle over the rice immediately before serving.

Khao Phad Mangsawirat

VEGETARIAN FRIED RICE

½ cup (125 g/4 oz) white or haricot beans
½ teaspoon salt
1 small onion, sliced
3 tablespoons vegetable oil
4 cups (750 g/1½ lb) cooked plain rice (page 32)
1 tablespoon light soya sauce
1 tablespoon Maggi sauce
½ cup (125 ml/4 fl oz) pineapple juice
1 cup (125 g/4 oz) pineapple cubes
¼ cup (40 g/1½ oz) raisins
1 green pepper (capsicum), cut into strips
1 tomato, diced
To serve:
1 cucumber, sliced
2 spring onions (scallions), sliced
1 lime

Soak the beans in cold water overnight. Drain, then cover with fresh water. Add salt, bring to the boil and simmer for 1 hour. Drain.

Fry the onion in the vegetable oil for 2-3 minutes. Then add the beans, rice, light soya sauce and Maggi sauce. Mix well and continue frying for another 2-3 minutes.

Add in the pineapple juice, pineapple cubes, raisins, green pepper and tomato. Fry on low heat for 3-5 minutes. Remove from the heat.

Garnish with the sliced cucumber and spring onions. Squeeze the lime over the rice before serving.

Phad Prikwan Kap Thua

GREEN PEPPER WITH WHITE BEANS

1 cup (250 g/8 oz) white or haricot beans
2 teaspoons salt
3 green peppers (capsicums)
3 tablespoons vegetable oil
2 tablespoons light soya sauce
1 tablespoon dark soya sauce
1 teaspoon sugar
1 tablespoon cornflour (cornstarch)
3 tablespoons water

Soak the beans in cold water overnight, drain then cover with fresh water. Add 1 teaspoon salt and bring to the boil. Simmer for 1 hour. Drain.

Cut the green peppers into pieces 1 cm (½ inch) wide and 2.5 cm (1 inch) long, removing the seeds and white membrane from inside.

Fry the peppers in the vegetable oil for 2-3 minutes and then add the beans, light soya sauce, dark soya sauce, 1 teaspoon salt and sugar. Continue frying for another 2-3 minutes.

Mix the cornflour with the water, add to the other ingredients, stir well for 1-2 minutes, then serve.

Thord Man Khao Phod

FRIED CORN CAKES

2 cups (350 g/12 oz) sweetcorn kernels
1 egg
1 tablespoon yellow curry paste (page 42)
2-3 tablespoons rice flour
2 tablespoons light soya sauce
1 teaspoon salt
3 tablespoons wheat flour
2 cups (450 ml/¾ pint) vegetable oil

Sauce:
4 tablespoons vinegar
4 tablespoons water
¼ cup (50 g/2 oz) sugar
1 teaspoon salt
½ chili, crushed
¼ cup (50 g/2 oz) peanuts
¼ cucumber, thinly sliced

Mix together the corn, egg, curry paste, rice flour, soya sauce and 1 teaspoon salt. Shape the mixture with your hands to form circular cakes about 2.5 cm (1 inch) in diameter.

Dip the cakes in the wheat flour and then fry immediately in the very hot oil. (Do not fry more than 6-8 cakes at a time or they will not cook properly).

To make the sauce, bring to the boil the vinegar, water, sugar, salt and chili. Let it cool.

Pound the peanuts and add to the cooled mixture. Lastly, add the cucumber.

Nam Prik Makhua Yao

MASHED AUBERGINES

5 shallots
2 aubergines (eggplants)
5 cloves garlic
1 fresh chili
1 teaspoon salt
2 tablespoons vegetable oil
2-3 eggs, hard-boiled
20 mint leaves

Peel the outer skin off the shallots and place them with the unpeeled aubergines, garlic cloves and chili under a hot grill or over a barbecue until browned. Peel the aubergines and garlic.

Pound the chili, shallots and garlic together. Then add the salt and aubergine and pound together again.

Fry the pounded mixture in the vegetable oil for 2-3 minutes. Remove from the heat. Cut the hard-boiled eggs into wedge shapes and mix in with the other ingredients or serve separately.

Sprinkle the aubergine with mint leaves and serve accompanied by vegetables.

Mashed Aubergines

Fried Corn Cakes served with a relish of chopped vegetables.

Phad Thua Song Kruang

FRIED BEANS WITH PUMPKIN

2 cups (500 g/1 lb) white or haricot beans
2 teaspoons salt
2 tablespoons dark soya sauce
1 clove garlic, crushed
2 tablespoons vegetable oil
125 g (4 oz) French beans
1 cup (150 g/5 oz) diced pumpkin
½ cup (125 ml/4 fl oz) water
3 tablespoons light soya sauce
1 tablespoon sugar
¼ cup (50 g/2 oz) sliced tomatoes

Soak the beans in cold water overnight, drain then cover with fresh water. Add salt, bring to the boil and simmer for 1 hour. Drain.

Mix the beans with the dark soya sauce and leave to stand for 15 minutes.

Fry the garlic in the vegetable oil. Cut the French beans into 1-cm (½-inch) pieces and add to the garlic with the pumpkin. Fry for 2-3 minutes and then add the water, light soya sauce, sugar, tomatoes and the haricot bean mixture. Cook for 5 minutes or until all the ingredients are cooked.

Carb Taohou Hed Fang

MUSHROOM AND BEANCURD SALAD

200 g (7 oz) mushrooms
1 medium square hard beancurd
½ teaspoon salt
½ teaspoon chopped dried chili
½ teaspoon chopped galangal
2 tablespoons lemon juice
1 tablespoon chopped coriander
1 tablespoon golden rice semolina (page 35)
1 tablespoon sliced onion
To serve:
1 lettuce
1 cup mint leaves
1 cucumber, sliced
1 small Chinese cabbage

Slice the mushrooms finely and cut the beancurd into strips.

Mix them together, adding the salt, chili and galangal, then the lemon juice, coriander, rice semolina and onion.

Arrange the lettuce leaves in the bottom of a serving dish, pile the mushroom mixture on top and garnish with the mint leaves.

The cucumber and cabbage are served as a side dish.

Tom Jued Si Khao

CHINESE CABBAGE SOUP WITH BEANCURD

2 medium squares soft beancurd
1 medium Chinese cabbage
1 cup (125g/4 oz) mushrooms
4 cups (1 litre/1¾ pints) water
½ teaspoon salt
1 tablespoon light soya sauce
1 teaspoon vinegar
½ teaspoon pepper

Cut the beancurd into small cubes, the cabbage into 2.5-cm (1-inch) pieces, and the mushrooms into halves.

Bring the water to the boil, then add the salt, light soya sauce, vinegar and cabbage. Simmer for 5 minutes before adding the beancurd, mushrooms and pepper. Simmer for a further 5 minutes or until the cabbage is tender.

Tom Yam Hed Mangsawirat

VEGETARIAN MUSHROOM SOUP

500 g (1 lb) mushrooms
5 fresh chilies
3 bergamot leaves
3 cups (750 ml/1¼ pints) water
3 tablespoons lemon juice
3 tablespoons light soya sauce
1 stem coriander

Cut the mushrooms into small pieces and slice the chilies lengthways. Bring the water to the boil and add the bergamot leaves and mushrooms. Simmer for 3 minutes or until the mushrooms are cooked.

Before serving, stir the lemon juice, soya sauce, coriander and chilies into the soup.

Tom Yam Kalampli Kathi

CABBAGE SOUP WITH COCONUT MILK

500 g (1 lb) cabbage
3 shallots
3 cloves garlic, chopped
2 dried red chilies, chopped
4 cups (1 litre/1¾ pt) coconut milk
3 tablespoons lemon juice
2-3 tablespoons light soya sauce
Garnish:
coriander leaves

Cut the cabbage into cubes not larger than 5 cm (2 inches). Place the whole peeled shallots in a hot oven (220°C/425°F/Gas Mark 7) or on foil over a barbecue or burner until slightly burnt. Then pound them with the garlic and chilies.

Bring the coconut milk to the boil and add the cabbage and pounded mixture to it. Allow to simmer for 10-12 minutes, or until the cabbage is tender.

Just before serving, stir in the lemon juice and soya sauce, and garnish with a few coriander leaves.

Soup Phak

VEGETABLE SOUP

1 onion sliced
2 tablespoons (25g/1 oz) margarine
1 medium Chinese cabbage
1 carrot, sliced
3 sticks celery, chopped
4 cups (1 litre/1¾ pints) water
1 teaspoon salt
½ teaspoon pepper

Fry the onion in the margarine for about 1 minute. Chop the cabbage and add to the onion with the carrot and celery. Fry for about 2 minutes. Put this vegetable mixture into a soup pot.

Add the water, salt and pepper. Cover and leave the soup to simmer for 1 hour, stirring from time to time.

Pour the soup through a strainer and serve only the strained liquid.

Tom Jued Normai Tao Hou

BEANCURD SOUP

3 medium squares soft beancurd
5 cups (1.25 litres/2 pints) water
½ cup (50 g/2 oz) sliced bamboo shoots
½ teaspoon salt
1 teaspoon light soya sauce
1 onion, chopped
1 tablespoon vegetable oil
1 teaspoon sesame oil
2 teaspoons finely chopped ginger
2 spring onions (scallions), sliced

Cut the beancurd into small cubes. Bring the water to the boil and add the bamboo shoots, salt and soya sauce. Leave to simmer while you fry the onion in the vegetable oil mixed with the sesame oil. When the onion is tender, add it to the soup and simmer for 5 minutes. Stir in the beancurd and ginger and simmer for a final 5 minutes before serving sprinkled with spring onions.

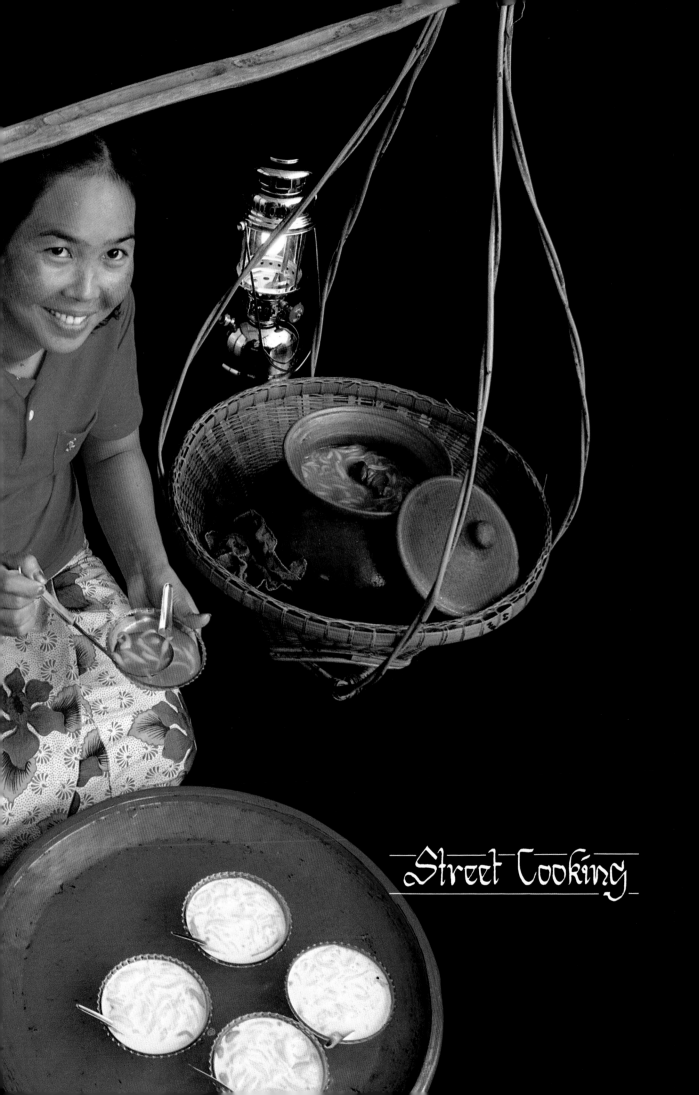

Street Cooking

Street Cooking

Some of the most varied street life in the world can be found along Bangkok's crowded, bustling pavements. It can be difficult for the pedestrian to find walking space between the stalls and vendors, but navigating among these obstacles is a feast for the senses. In particular, one's taste buds are constantly tempted by the "fast food" Thai-style, served at open-air stands which flourish all over the city. There are makeshift counters, pots balanced precariously on shoulder poles, noodle barrows submerged beneath myriad utensils and ingredients. Charcoal burners are used for steaming and barbecuing. Glass cabinets display a multitude of different kinds of noodles; chickens and spiced ducks suspended at eye-level; as well as bowls of sliced pork, diced fish, prawns and mussels. These kitchenettes on wheels and poles offer mouth-watering arrays of sweet and savoury snacks. On the waterways, little boats manoeuvre from dwelling to dwelling, similarly transformed into mobile kitchens.

Everything is carefully prepared in advance so that in most cases the food only needs reheating. If you order "kuoy tiaw", in a matter of minutes the noodles are tossed into the hot stock, retrieved with a special long-handled sieve, poured into a bowl with pork or prawns, and seasoned with sauce and fresh coriander. "Khao phad", or fried rice, is wrapped in that perfect natural packaging, the banana leaf, which is sold cut to all sizes at markets. The street chefs are a joy to watch, as they skilfully concoct a range of subtle dishes — folding rice pancakes as fine as gauze, carving pineapples into stars.

When a vendor arrives in a soi, or lane, he calls out his wares. The fruit seller is one of the first to appear, crying "som o", "som kheo wan", "maprao phao" or "sapparod", according to the season. Next comes the flower and garland merchant shouting "puang malai" to householders, who hurry forth to purchase offerings for their spirit houses.

The ice cream vendor has no need to call out as his cart is hung with little glass bells, which tinkle his arrival to the children. The most impressive of all is the noodle seller, with his barrow sagging beneath the weight of its contents. He slowly makes his way along the soi, tapping "tok tok, tok tok" on a bamboo pole. Cries of "khanom cha" announce the last of the vendors to make an appearance, the sweets seller. She displays confections of milk and coconut cream, and tropical pastel-coloured jellies called "agar-agar". And thus, throughout the day, people can satisfy their hunger without leaving home, and without lighting their own stoves.

The recipes in this chapter have been adapted to home-cooking conditions to enable you to try some of the street vendors' dishes in your own kitchen. The photographs also show the food presented as it might be on your table, not as the street vendor would hand it to you!

The Thais eat these snacks and sweetmeats at any time of the day or night, for they are inveterate snackers. Hors d'oeuvres before a meal or at a cocktail party do not feature in Thai life, and desserts, other than fresh fruit, are not usually served at the end of a meal. However, the recipes included here will adapt well to Western habits. The savoury dishes would be ideal as hors d'oeuvres or on the buffet table, and the sweet dishes — usually based on coconut cream — make unusual desserts.

Kai Ping Phanang

SKEWERED CHICKEN WITH PHANANG CURRY

750 g (1½ lb) chicken breast
1½ cups (350 ml/12 fl oz) coconut milk
2 tablespoons phanang curry paste (page 43)
1 tablespoon fish sauce
2 large sugar cubes
Garnish:
1 cucumber, sliced
4 sprigs basil

15 bamboo or metal skewers

Slice the chicken breast and thread it onto the skewers.

For the sauce, bring a third of the coconut milk to the boil, and simmer until a skin forms on the surface. Add the curry paste, fish sauce and sugar.

Place the chicken under a hot grill or over a charcoal barbecue until the chicken is hot. Soak the hot chicken in the sauce for 15 minutes, then continue to grill, basting with the rest of the coconut milk, until cooked through.

Serve, garnished with the cucumber and basil.

Khanom Pang Nah Kung

PRAWN TOAST

500 g (1 lb) prawns (shrimp), shelled
1 thick slice ham, diced
1 teaspoon ground coriander root
4 tablespoons breadcrumbs
3 eggs
pepper
1 teaspoon salt
1 small loaf sliced bread
oil for deep-frying

Chop the prawns finely and mix them with the ham, coriander, breadcrumbs and 1 egg. Add salt and pepper to taste. Beat the other 2 eggs in a separate bowl.

Spread the prawn mixture on the slices of bread. Cut the bread into small squares.

Dip the bread in the beaten egg and fry with the prawn mixture facing down in the deep hot oil.

When golden brown, remove and drain on kitchen paper.

Serve with Cucumber Sauce (Ajad).

Luk Nua

MIXED MEAT PATTIES

4 cloves garlic, crushed
2 tablespoons finely chopped onion
3 coriander roots, chopped
10 black peppercorns
300 g (10 oz) pork, minced or ground
300 g (10 oz) beef, minced or ground
2 eggs, beaten
fish sauce to taste
oil for frying

Pound or grind the garlic, onion, coriander root and peppercorns together to form a thick paste. Add the meat, eggs and fish sauce. Mix well.

Form the mixture into 6-8 patties, like hamburgers, and fry them in the hot oil for about 5 minutes or until cooked through.

Eggs with Tamarind Sauce

Stuffed Omelette with rice and a tomato sauce.

Khai Look Koey

Khai Yad Sai

EGGS WITH TAMARIND SAUCE

4 tablespoons sugar
2 tablespoons tamarind juice
3 tablespoons fish sauce
3 shallots, chopped
2 tablespoons oil
10 hard-boiled eggs
15 coriander leaves
1 red pepper (capsicum)

Bring to the boil the sugar, tamarind juice and fish sauce. Simmer until it thickens.

Brown the shallots in the oil, then drain, reserving the oil in the pan.

Shell the eggs and sauté in the hot oil until golden all over.

Halve the eggs and arrange them in a serving dish. Pour the sauce over and garnish with the coriander leaves, shallots and slivers of red pepper.

STUFFED OMELETTE

1 medium potato
1 small carrot
salt
2 cloves garlic, crushed
oil for frying
200 g (7 oz) pork, minced or ground
1 small tomato, diced
1 small onion, chopped
1 teaspoon light soya sauce
pepper
4 fresh eggs
1 tablespoon milk
Garnish:
coriander sprig

Cook the peeled potato and carrot in boiling salted water then drain. Dice the potato, and slice the carrot into rings.

Brown the garlic in oil, and then add the meat and vegetables. Sauté for a few minutes. Add the soya sauce, salt and pepper and stir well. Remove from the heat.

Beat the eggs with the milk and pour them into another, lightly oiled, hot frying pan. When the omelette begins to set, put the meat and vegetable mixture in the centre, and fold the sides of the omelette over to form a square.

Turn the omelette over like a pancake, to brown the other side. Garnish. If individual omelettes are preferred, cook in batches.

Chicken Satay with Satay Sauce and other relishes.

Satéh Kai

CHICKEN SATAY

750 g (1½ lb) chicken breast
1 stalk lemon grass, finely chopped
5 bergamot leaves, finely chopped
5 shallots, chopped
1 tablespoon coriander seeds
½ cup (125 ml/4 fl oz) milk
2 tablespoons light soya sauce
Garnish (optional):
curly spring onions (scallions) page 22

15 small wooden or metal skewers

Slice the chicken breast finely. Pound together or blend in a blender, the lemon grass, bergamot, shallots and coriander, adding a little milk to produce a smooth paste. Add the rest of the milk and the soya sauce and blend again or mix well.

Pour the mixture into a large bowl, and add the chicken slices.

Marinate for 15 minutes, then thread the chicken slices onto the skewers. Place over a charcoal barbecue or under a hot grill, turning once, for 5-6 minutes or until cooked through. Garnish with curly spring onions, if liked, and serve with Satay Sauce (Nam Jim Sateh).

Khai Tun

THAI STEAMED EGGS

2 eggs
2 tablespoons minced or ground pork
1 teaspoon fish sauce
½ cup (125 ml/4 fl oz) stock
1 spring onion (scallion), chopped
pepper
salt

Beat the eggs together. Add the other ingredients and beat again.

Pour into a bain marie or into a heatproof bowl and place that in a pan of boiling water. Cover the pan. Control the heat so that the water in the pan is just simmering, and steam the eggs gently for 5-10 minutes or until set.

Ma Hor

PINEAPPLE WITH PORK AND PEANUTS

½ cup (125 g/4 oz) minced or ground pork
2 tablespoons chopped garlic
2 tablespoons chopped shallots
3 tablespoons oil
1 tablespoon powdered dried shrimp
1 teaspoon finely chopped ginger
2 tablespoons crushed peanuts
1 tablespoon sugar
1 tablespoon fish sauce
1 teaspoon lemon juice
1 pineapple
Garnish:
coriander leaves
1 red pepper (capsicum)

Sauté the pork until browned without using any oil. Put aside.

Brown the garlic and the shallots separately in the oil until crisp. Add them to the pork.

Add the powdered shrimp, ginger, peanuts, sugar, fish sauce and lemon juice, and mix well.

Peel and slice the pineapple. Cut the slices into small triangles. On each triangle place a ball of the pork mixture, half a coriander leaf and a strip of the red pepper.

Ma Hor Som

ORANGES WITH PORK AND PEANUTS

4 oranges
stuffing as above

Peel and quarter the oranges. Make a slit in the back of each quarter and in the slit place 1 teaspoon of the stuffing used in Pineapple with Pork and Peanuts (Ma Hor).

Thod Mun Kung

PRAWN CAKES

500 g (1 lb) prawns (shrimp), shelled
4 cloves garlic
4 coriander roots
salt
pepper
oil for deep-frying

Mince or grind the prawns. Pound the garlic, coriander, salt and pepper together to form a thick paste.

Mix the minced prawns with this paste and form the mixture into flat cakes, about 5 mm (¼ inch) thick.

Bring the oil to the boil over high heat then lower the heat. Fry the prawn cakes until lightly browned. Drain and serve.

Khao Niaw Na Kung

STICKY RICE WITH PRAWNS

350 g (12 oz) prawns (shrimp), shelled
1 cup (75 g/3 oz) grated coconut
1 teaspoon ground coriander root
1 teaspoon pepper
3 tablespoons oil
2 teaspoons salt
2 tablespoons sugar
3 cups (500 g/1 lb) sticky coconut rice (page 32)
Garnish:
2 tablespoons chopped bergamot leaves

Chop up the prawns and mix them with the coconut.

Brown the coriander with the pepper in the oil, then add the prawns and coconut. Sauté, stirring for about 3 minutes or until the prawns turn pink. Mix in the salt and sugar.

Serve the sticky rice in individual dishes with the prawn mixture on top. Sprinkle with the bergamot.

Khanom Jeeb Sai Kai

CHICKEN RAVIOLI

Dough:
1½ cups (250 g/8 oz) rice flour
1 tablespoon wheat flour
2 tablespoons sticky rice flour
1½ cups (350 ml/12 fl oz) water
2 tablespoons oil
2 tablespoons tapioca flour
Filling:
3 cloves garlic, crushed
1 teaspoon ground coriander root
1 teaspoon pepper
4 tablespoons oil
500 g (1 lb) chicken meat, finely chopped
125 g (4 oz) onion, chopped
4 tablespoons crushed peanuts
1 tablespoon sugar
3 tablespoons fish sauce
Garnish:
3 small chilies, sliced
coriander leaves

Leaving aside 2 tablespoons of the rice flour, mix the first 5 ingredients together in a pan. Cook over medium heat, stirring, until a large ball forms.

Remove from the heat and allow to cool a little. Sprinkle with the remaining rice and tapioca flours. Knead well and then cover the dough with a damp cloth.

To make the filling, brown the crushed garlic and coriander root with the pepper in the oil. Add the chicken, onion, peanuts, sugar and fish sauce. Cook over medium heat, stirring continually, until the mixture boils down and becomes drier. Remove from the heat and leave to cool.

Form the dough into small balls. Flatten these into thin rounds. Place a little filling in the centre of half of the rounds and use the other rounds as lids. Seal the edges by pressing with a fork. Steam for 10 minutes.

Serve garnished with chilies and coriander leaves.

Khao Krìab Pak Morh

STEAMED RICE PANCAKES WITH PORK

Batter:
1½ cups (250 g/8 oz) rice flour
4 tablespoons tapioca flour
2 cups (450 ml/¾ pint) water
Filling:
1 tablespoon crushed garlic
1 tablespoon chopped coriander root
1 teaspoon pepper
2 tablespoons oil
200 g (7 oz) pork, minced or ground
3 tablespoons palm sugar
2 tablespoons fish sauce
125 g (4 oz) turnip, grated
4 tablespoons water
1 onion, finely sliced
½ cup (50 g/2 oz) crushed peanuts
coriander leaves

Mix the 2 kinds of flour with the water to produce the pancake batter.

For the filling brown the crushed garlic and coriander root with the pepper in the oil. Add the pork and sauté for 3-4 minutes until browned. Remove the pork mixture from the pan and reserve.

In the same frying pan, mix the sugar, fish sauce, turnip and water. Bring to the boil and stir until the mixture boils down and becomes drier. Add the pork mixture, onion and peanuts and mix in well. Cook for 5 minutes. Remove from the heat.

The only successful way to cook rice pancakes is by steaming. Half fill a fairly deep, flameproof container or saucepan with water. Stretch a piece of muslin or cotton over the top like a drum and tie down tightly with string. Place the pan over medium heat. When the steam appears through the material, spread a fine layer of batter over it. Cover with a lid for a minute and the pancake is cooked.

Place a tablespoon of the pork mixture in the centre of the pancake. Top the mixture with coriander leaves, then fold over the sides of the pancake to form a square parcel.

Repeat with the rest of the batter and pork mixture. Golden garlic in oil (see page 34), can be served with this dish.

Steamed Rice Pancakes with Pork; Pork Tapioca Balls.

Sakhou Sai Mou

PORK TAPIOCA BALLS

Filling:
1 tablespoon chopped garlic
1 teaspoon chopped coriander root
1 teaspoon pepper
2 tablespoons oil
200 g (7 oz) pork, minced or ground
3 tablespoons palm sugar
2 tablespoons fish sauce
125 g (4 oz) turnip, grated
4 tablespoons water
1 onion, finely chopped
½ cup (50 g/2 oz) crushed peanuts
Dough:
1½ cups (250 g/8 oz) tapioca flour
4 tablespoons hot water
To serve:
3 tablespoons golden garlic in oil (page 34)
coriander leaves, chopped
lettuce leaves

Brown the garlic and coriander with the pepper in the oil. Add the pork. Sauté for 2-3 minutes until browned, then remove from the pan and put aside.

In the same pan, mix together the sugar, fish sauce, turnip and water. Boil down until the mixture becomes drier, stirring all the time. Add the pork mixture, onion and peanuts. Mix well and cook for 5 minutes. Remove from the heat.

Mix the tapioca with the hot water and knead the dough. Shape it into small balls and then flatten them to produce round pancakes.

Place a small quantity of the pork mixture in the centre of each tapioca round, and bring together the edges to form a ball. Steam the balls for 15 minutes.

Serve with lettuce and a selection of Thai sauces and accompaniments.

Por Pia Kung

PRAWN PANCAKES

500 g (1 lb) prawns (shrimp), shelled
1 thick slice ham
1 teaspoon sugar
1 teaspoon salt
pepper
½ cup (50 g/2 oz) wheat flour
20 rice pancakes (page 136)
coriander leaves
oil for frying
Garnish:
½ pineapple, diced
1 cucumber, sliced
1 pepper (capsicum), sliced

Chop the prawns and ham finely and mix with the sugar and salt. Add pepper to taste.

Mix the flour with just enough water to form a stiff paste.

Prepare the pancakes as for Steamed Rice Pancakes with Pork (Khao Kriab Pak Morh) on page 136, but keep them small – about 7.5 cm (3 inches) in diameter. Place a little of the prawn mixture in the centre of half the pancakes and sprinkle with coriander leaves. Spread the paste round the edge and place another pancake on top of each to act as a lid. Press the edges firmly together.

Brown the pancakes in the oil over medium heat.

Serve garnished with the pineapple, cucumber and pepper.

Khao Niaw Nah Krachik

STICKY RICE WITH COCONUT SAUCE

1 cup (250 ml/8 fl oz) jasmine water
1½ cups (350 g/12 oz) palm sugar
2 cups (175 g/6 oz) grated coconut
3 cups (500 g/1 lb) sticky coconut rice (page 32)

Mix the jasmine water and sugar in a pan. Bring to the boil over medium heat. Reduce the heat and stir in the coconut. Simmer until the liquid has reduced, stirring from time to time. When the sauce is thick, remove it from the heat and leave to cool.

Pour this sauce over the sticky coconut rice. (In Thailand, this sauce is flavoured with the perfume of a special candle. The candle is placed in the pan, lit and then extinguished. The pan is covered for a few minutes to allow the smoke to permeate the sauce).

Sang Khaya

COCONUT CUSTARD

5 eggs
1 cup (250 ml/8 fl oz) coconut cream
1 cup (250 g/8 oz) sugar

Beat the eggs with the coconut cream and sugar until the mixture is frothy.

Pour the liquid into small moulds. Place in a steamer over boiling water, cover and cook for about 20 minutes or until the mixture has set.

Kluey Chezam

COCONUT BANANAS

6-9 bananas
2 cups (450 ml/¾ pint) water
1½ cups (350 g/12 oz) sugar
½ cup (125 ml/4 fl oz) coconut cream
½ teaspoon salt

Peel the bananas. If they are large cut them in half across, but if you are using small bananas leave them whole. You can also make decorative cuts in them.

Mix the water with the sugar, and bring to the boil, stirring. Simmer for 5 minutes.

Add the bananas and cook for 5 minutes. Drain.

Bring the coconut cream to the boil with the salt. Reduce the heat and stir until the liquid thickens.

Serve the bananas in or with the warm coconut cream.

Khao Niaw Mamuang

MANGOES WITH STICKY RICE

1 cup (250 ml/8 fl oz) coconut cream
1 tablespoon sugar
1 teaspoon salt
4 ripe mangoes
3 cups (500 g/1 lb) sticky coconut rice (page 32)

Mix the coconut cream with the sugar and salt, and bring to the boil. Simmer for a few minutes, stirring occasionally.

Peel the mangoes and slice them, removing the stones. Arrange the mangoes on individual plates with rice beside them. Spoon the sauce over the rice.

Mangoes with Sticky Rice

Coconut Bananas

Floating Lotus Seeds with some melon and mango balls to add colour.

FLOATING LOTUS SEEDS

Bua Loy

3 cups (500 g/1 lb) sticky rice flour
water
4 cups (1 litre/1¾ pints) coconut cream
2 cups (500 g/1 lb) sugar
1 teaspoon salt
To decorate (optional):
flower petals

Mix the rice flour with just enough water to make a stiff paste. Knead well and then form into pea-sized balls.

Bring a large pan of water to the boil. Toss in the balls, and take them out when they float on the surface. Drain.

Mix half the coconut cream with 1 cup (250 ml/8 fl oz) water, the sugar and salt. Bring to the boil and add the flour balls. When the mixture returns to the boil, remove from the heat and stir in the remaining coconut cream.

Serve as a dessert in small bowls. Decorate with petals, if liked.

INDEX

142

ACKNOWLEDGEMENTS

The traditional art of fruit and vegetable carving.

The authors, photographer and publishers would like to
thank for their help, Miss Suzan Croft, Mr and Mrs Suthipan Chirativat,
Mrs Adela Turin, Mr Albert Coindat, Mr Donald Gibson of Mengrai Kilns,
Khun Chaiwut Tulayadhan of Neold, Mr and Mrs Guido Secchi,
and the management and staff of the Regent hotel, Bangkok,
particularly M.R. Chirisuda Vuttigrai, Mr Gregoire Salamin and
Khun Phachongchit Phithaksakorn.

The photographs of the dishes were taken at the Regent hotel, Bangkok.